ALICE FREEMAN PALMER

Portrait in 1892

THE LIFE OF ALICE FREEMAN PALMER

BY

GEORGE HERBERT PALMER

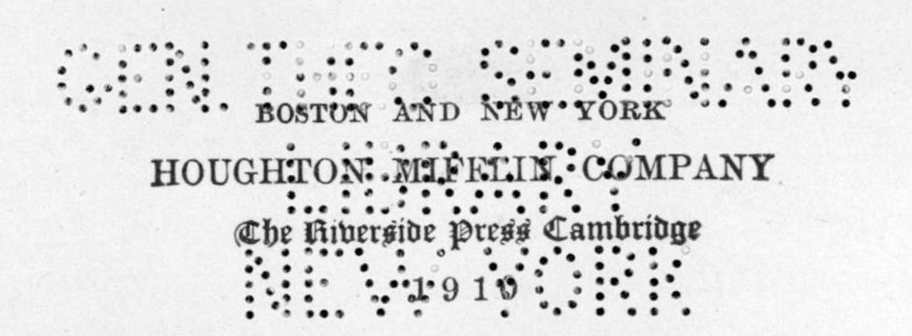

BOSTON AND NEW YORK
HOUGHTON MIFFLIN COMPANY
The Riverside Press Cambridge
1910

Published April 1908

SEVENTEENTH IMPRESSION

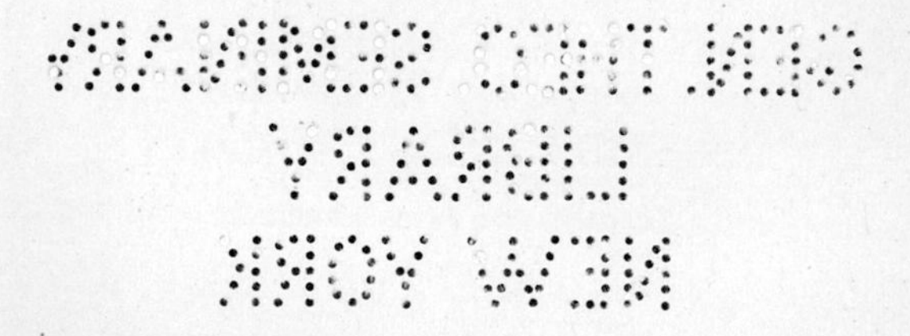

CONTENTS

ILLUSTRATIONS

ALICE FREEMAN PALMER

When fell, to-day, the word that she had gone,
Not this my thought: Here a bright journey ends,
Here rests a soul unresting; here, at last,
Here ends that earnest strength, that generous life —
For all her life was giving. Rather this
I said (after the first swift, sorrowing pang):
Radiant with love, and love's unending power,
Hence, on a new quest, starts an eager spirit —
No dread, no doubt, unhesitating forth
With asking eyes; pure as the bodiless souls
Whom poets vision near the central throne
Angelically ministrant to man;
So fares she forth with smiling, Godward face;
Nor should we grieve, but give eternal thanks —
Save that we mortal are, and needs must mourn.

RICHARD WATSON GILDER.

December 6, 1902.

THE LIFE OF ALICE FREEMAN PALMER

I

INTRODUCTION

THREE reasons impel me to write this book, affection first of all. Mrs. Palmer was my wife, deeply beloved and honored. Whatever perpetuates that honor brings me peace. To leave the dead wholly dead is rude. Vivid creature that she was, she must not lie forgotten. Something of her may surely be saved if only I have skill. Perhaps my grateful pen may bring to others a portion of the bounty I myself received.

A second and more obvious summons comes from the fact that in herself and apart from me Mrs. Palmer was a notable person. Somebody therefore may be tempted to write her life if I do not; for her friends were numbered by the ten thousand. At her death I received nearly two thousand letters from statesmen, schoolgirls, clerks, lawyers, teachers, country wives, outcasts, millionaires, ministers, men of letters, — a heterogeneous and to me largely an unknown company, but alike in feeling the marvel of her personality and the loss her death had caused them. Few women of her time, I have come to think, were more widely loved. And now these persons are recalling her influence and asking for explanation. Where lay that strange power, and how did she obtain it? She lived no longer than most of us. She had no early advantage of birth, physical vigor, or station. Half her years were passed in comparative poverty. During only nine did she hold positions which could be called conspicuous. She wrote little. In no field of scholarship was she eminent. Her tastes were domestic, her voice gentle, her disposition feminine and self-effacing. Yet by personal power rather than by favoring circumstance this woman sent out an influence from the Atlantic to the Pacific, an influence unique in kind and puzzling those on whom it fell. In her appearance there was nothing enigmatic. Altogether simple she seemed, approachable, playful even, interested in common things, in common people, with no air of profundity, and small inclination to remake after her own pattern the characters of those who came near; but any one on whom she turned her great eyes went out from her presence renewed. Hope revived, one's special powers were heightened; the wise, the exalted course became suddenly easy; while toil and difficulties began to spice the life they had previously soured. In all this there was something mysterious which I am solicited to explain.

I cannot explain it. Probably genius is never explicable. The more nearly it is examined, the more intricately marvelous it appears. Fifteen years of closest companionship with Mrs. Palmer did not disclose to me the pulse of that curious machine. She always remained a surprise. Yet I never tired of studying her; for though we seldom can fully comprehend a person, in studying one who is great we can push analysis farther than elsewhere and with larger entertainment and profit; we discover a multitude of ingredients unsuspected at first; and, most interesting of all, we come upon strange modes of turning trivial things to power and of gaily discarding what men usually count important. And even when at last we arrive at what defies analysis, being the very individuality itself, its beautiful mystery still lures us on and — like Keats's Grecian Urn — enlargingly "teases us out of thought."

Accordingly, in response to many requests, I mean to make the second object of this book the study of an attractive human problem, even though by doing so I prove to how limited an extent the demand for an understanding can be gratified. I certainly shall never succeed in accounting for Mrs. Palmer's charm; I fear I shall not even reproduce it. In her lifetime many artists tried to depict that haunting and variable face, but without success. The sun itself gave only partial and contradictory reports. So I must fail in setting forth so elusive a being. But this failure will restrain less familiar hands; and I can at least set in order the chief facts of her life and select characteristic specimens of her sayings and writings.

And if so much is accomplished, perhaps I may accomplish something more. In life Mrs. Palmer's personality was an influential one. It embodied stimulating ideals. Those who approached her, even casually, gained power and peace. President Tucker says, "There is no other of our generation, with the possible exception of Phillips Brooks, who has stood to such a degree for those qualities in which we must all believe with unquenchable faith if we are to do anything in this world." And President Eliot, "To my mind this career is unmatched by that of any other American woman. Mrs. Palmer's life and labors are the best example thus far set before American womanhood." If my portrait of her, then, is correct, invigoration will go forth from it and disheartened souls be cheered; for after all, her modes of life — with suitable adaptation to alien temperaments — are capable of pretty wide application. What was peculiar in her was small. She chiefly distinguished herself by wise ways of confronting the usual world. While, then, I try to restore her to life for the benefit of those who did and did not know her, I may hope that readers will find in the disclosure of her methods material for their own strength and courage.

One more aim remains, weighty, yet lying on the surface. In some of the social movements of her time Mrs. Palmer had a considerable share. During her life education was undergoing reconstruction, new colleges were coming into existence, fresh opportunities and capacities for women were being claimed and tested. It is well to follow such movements in the lives of their leaders and to understand the situation in which those leaders found themselves. By sharing in their early hopes, difficulties, and results, we comprehend better the world we inhabit. As Mrs. Palmer was sometimes forced into such leadership, she may be said to have a certain historical importance.

Such, then, are the three impulses of this book,— the insatiability of love, the general desire for portraiture, the rights of history. Here personal, psychological, social motives mingle. Since I can no longer talk with her, I would talk of her and get the comfort of believing that even now without me she may not be altogether perfect. Enjoying, too, artistic criticism, psychology, ethical problems, I gladly bring my special knowledge to bear on what many found mysterious, pleasing myself with thinking that in making her known to old friends and new I shall also make them better known to themselves. And then, retaining my belief in the public causes for which she stood, I should like briefly to record their history and thus encourage the next generation in its own way to push them on. But in carrying out these collective aims I encounter obstacles which rigidly limit my success.

Mrs. Palmer was a person of strong temperamental reserve. One did not at first suspect it. She seemed uncommonly open; and so indeed she was — open for going forth to others, but not for admitting them to her. Her simple manners and generous sympathies put every one at ease and gave each the satisfaction, entirely well-grounded, of feeling that he was for the moment her greatest object of regard. But when one turned about and tried to make her the object of regard, one did not penetrate far. Not that she had the distrustful modesty which fears to talk of its doings. She knew her powers, respected them, and had a good deal of the child's way of finding herself as interesting as did others. Nor did she, like an aristocrat, seek to screen herself from the common gaze. But accustomed as she was to ministering and not being ministered unto, the loving scrutiny which most were eager to bestow she took, as it were, merely in passing. Nothing was easier than a superficial acquaintance with her; but friends have told me that after an acquaintance of five years, while admiring devotion steadily grew, they knew her no better than on the first day. The springs of her conduct, what she cared for most, her ultimate beliefs and allegiances, few could know — perhaps not even herself.

It is difficult to penetrate far into a nature so concrete and unconscious, a nature, too, which held itself aloof from others by perpetual kindness. To depict it I might seem obliged to adopt an objective method and to allow the facts of the life to speak for themselves. But such a method would be useless; the life was uneventful. Hers was in general a smooth existence, in which little happened which might not befall any of us. I have often thought that God, Nature, Fate, or whoever the presiding power may be, foreseeing her desire always to find her happiness in that of others, provided her abundantly out of the common lot and left the element of distinction to be added by herself. It was always she who ennobled her circumstance. The occurrences of her life were few and unimportant, while what she drew from them fashioned a powerful personality. On herself, then, I must concentrate attention and try to induce my readers to look rather through the facts than at them. Of exciting narrative I have not much to offer. My book will be a kind of character novel, in which little occurs and nobody appears except the heroine.

And since I am detailing difficulties, let me say that my material is not quite what I should wish. I knew Mrs. Palmer during little more than a third of her life, when the formative influences of childhood and early womanhood were already absorbed into structure. My knowledge of these I piece together from what can be gathered from the few survivors of those early years and from incidental remarks of her own. But she was never reminiscent or introspective, had little interest in tracing her growth, and at any time took herself pretty much as she found herself. I once induced her to set down the principal dates of her life, and these notes now furnish the trusty framework of my tale. But as I am trying to construct an inner history rather than an outer, such a record goes only a little way. What I want is sayings and writings, so that my readers may catch her quality from her own lips; and these I lack in the midst of peculiar abundance. Let both that abundance and that lack reveal her character.

While she wrote no books and published only half a dozen articles, during each of her later years she made no less than twenty speeches. I at first thought I might exhibit her in extracts from these and from her letters. But each source I find to be only slenderly available. Her addresses were never written. Indeed, she seldom drew up memoranda of the points to be discussed. Her rapid speech confounded the reporters, so that in only a few instances have I reports which are anything like verbatim. Little, therefore, of her literary output remains, except what lodged in the minds of the hearers. There was in her a wastefulness like that of the blossoming tree. It sometimes disturbed me, and for it I occasionally took her to task. "Why will you," I said, "give all this time to speaking before uninstructed audiences, to discussions in endless committees with people too dull to know whether they are talking to the point, and to anxious interviews with tired and tiresome women? You would exhaust yourself less in writing books of lasting consequence. At present you are building no monument. When you are gone people will ask who you were, and nobody will be able to say." But I always received the same indifferent answer: "Well, why should they say? I am trying to make girls wiser and happier. Books don't help much toward that. They are entertaining enough, but really dead things. Why should I make more of them? It is people that count. You want to put yourself into people; they touch other people; these, others still, and so you go on working forever." I could never stir her interest in posthumous fame nor shake her estimate of the importance of dealing with individual human beings. Instinctively she adopted the idea of Jesus that if you would remould the world, the wise way is not to write, but to devote your fleeting years to persistent talks with a dozen young fishermen. And that this audacious method was effective in her small degree, as in that majestic instance, I now daily perceive as I meet with those who once were almost dead and were brought to living fruitfulness by her ardent patience. Yet still I mourn that through behaving so generously she largely disappeared.

It might seem that her letters would save her. They went forth by the hundred a week. They were usually written by her own hand, were long, careful, and highly personal, even when relating to business affairs. In them she expressed her best qualities. Whoever received one knew that it was a thing of value. In these, then, would naturally be found the material for her biography.

But the trait which I have just mentioned limits their use. She was unceasingly and minutely personal. The individual human being was in her world the all-important thing; and when she wrote him, every sentence concerned just him and no one else. This made her letters not merely unsuitable to print, but for the general reader unintelligible and for the most part uninteresting. She entered into her correspondent's circumstances with such specific detail as to bewilder any one who knew them less than she and he. To explain the allusions would require a letter longer than her own. His family ties, his business perplexities, his previous falls or rises, the wisest steps by which he may now reach his ends, the assurance that some one cares for his success and is elated over his little advancements — these are the matters of which she hourly wrote. Her eager simple language awoke his confidence and gratitude, but a different person would find her pages as empty as the newspaper of a neighboring town. Rarely do her letters contain general truths, discussions of public questions, opinions on books or persons, rarely do they relate to interests of her own. She has no interests which are not those of him to whom she writes. Even her occasional descriptions, like those sent home during her residences abroad, animated though they are and skilful in seizing the distinctive features of unaccustomed scenes, seem written because the reader needs to hear rather than she to speak. The notion of giving to somebody was a necessary factor in all she did and said. The artist craves expression primarily for delivering his own soul; knowing too that if he accomplishes this, he fixes public attention on his product. Her abounding soul sought neither that relief nor that approval, but found its full delight in relieving the souls of others.

Only once, so far as I know, did she turn to expression for her own sake. After her death I came upon a book of verses, written by her during the last five years of her life. She had given it the title of

"A Marriage Cycle," and in it had endeavored to mark the successive steps through which love brings a pair into union with each other, with nature, and with God. Marriage she had always reverenced, holding that only through it can either man or woman reach the largest fulfilment. When, comparatively late in life, she came to her own, she began in her usual fashion to bring out its inner significance and beauty. Romance was in her case no product of novelty, but was usually fertilized and rendered more exuberant by the deposits of time. Accordingly, when ten years of marriage and her own fortieth year were passed, wonder and gratitude over her happy condition became almost oppressive. From occasional dates scattered through this book of verses I judge she now began to snatch brief intervals from business and employ them for recording typical situations of crisis and growth in our life together. She had never written poetry before, though ever a student of it. Now she wrote purely for herself, rarely showing me anything. This book, more than any document that has survived her, depicts her heart, mind, courage, and character. For this reason I cannot use it. Its poetry is too intimate to be published during my life. Only a few pieces, expressing chiefly religious trust, I printed in a magazine shortly after her death. A few more, relating to country scenes, are given here in my thirteenth chapter.

Such then are my resources, my difficulties, and my aims. I move within restricted bounds. On account of an extremely individual quality, not much of Mrs. Palmer's poetry or correspondence can be used to illustrate her life. Still less is available of that which made her most widely known, her public speeches. The events of her life were not unusual, while her personality was baffling, sheltered as it was by instinctive reserve and too large to be easily measured. Yet such difficulties do not block the way; they merely define it. While rendering anything like the usual "Life and Letters" impossible, they point directly to something not less interesting, and perhaps of equal value: to an impressionistic portrait, a personal estimate, an evolutional study. For in calling her life uneventful I do not mean that it lacked interest. Every week was full of it, for herself and for others. To a discerning eye wealth of incident offers no such interest as an even unfolding brings, where event links with event, each later disclosing what was contained in germ in some earlier, until when, in orderly sequence, something is reached which under other circumstances might be astonishing, it comes prepared for and as only a matter of happy course. These are the truly dramatic lives, and such was preëminently hers. We follow here a harmoniously developed and stimulating drama, into which little that is accidental intrudes. To say that Mrs. Palmer was born in an obscure border village and became the renowned president of an eastern college at twenty-six may at first startle, but only until acquaintance with her shows how naturally this eminence and obscurity went together. In some degree to bring about that acquaintance and to set forth the orderly development of a noble nature is my inviting task.

And for an undertaking thus limited the material is not insufficient. There are my seventeen years of acquaintance, the recollections of those who were with her in early years, the talk of hundreds of students, the records of colleges and societies, the enthusiastic affection which everywhere attended her, and the marks of her influence still discernible in a multitude of lives. I have already mentioned the set of dates which she herself drew up. And then her letters, though on the whole of small historical value, contain precious illustrations of character. Everywhere they bear marks of her ardor, ease, sympathy, and elevation. They show, too, the growth of her powers. I use them often, therefore, but always with the aim of exhibiting herself, and not events or persons. For this reason no one of them is printed entire, no dates are affixed, nor names of those to whom they were written. Careless of the original text, I merely gather groups of characteristic fragments, sometimes even piecing together two which happen to be marked with a similar mood of mind.

My general plan will be to devote a single chapter to each definable section of her career; in it to analyze the forces which were then shaping her growth, and at its close, through these fragmentary letters or those of friends, to give an independent report of how she looked and spoke at the time. In this way I believe my scanty materials will yield their utmost. Possibly, too, the course of her development will be followed more readily if I mark out in it four unequal periods and give them special names. The first we may call her Family Life, extending up to her entering Windsor Academy in 1865; the second, the Expansion of her Powers, up to her graduation from Michigan University in 1876; the third, her Service of Others, up to her marriage in 1887; and last the Expression of Herself, up to her death in 1902. While these periods are not exclusive of one another, each is dominated by special interests which pretty clearly distinguish it, the later ones being hardly possible without those which go before. But Mrs. Palmer herself was unaware of any such divisions of her life; and if the reader chooses to forget them or to count them pedantic, I shall not think him disrespectful to me or to her.

In reference to one feature of my book a little warning may be well. This is a prejudiced story.

I am far from a dispassionate, or even a detached observer of her whom I would make known. She and I had become pretty completely one. Often my only way of telling about her is to tell about myself. The book, therefore, while ostensibly a biography, claims many privileges of an autobiography, and might properly enough be called the autobiography of a friend. In it I must be allowed abundant egotism, reminiscence, admiration, personal disclosure. But perhaps such a compound method will not be thought inappropriate in a portrait of one whose constant habit it was to mingle her abounding life with that of others.

II

CHILDHOOD

Alice Elvira Freeman was born on the night of February 21, 1855, at Colesville, Broome County, New York. The influences which chiefly shaped her childhood were her country life, her narrow means, and her father's change of occupation. All else is subordinate to these.

Colesville is rather a collection of farms than of houses, Windsor, its nearest considerable village, being seven miles away; its nearest town, Binghamton, a dozen miles from Windsor. All the child's early years were passed in a tract of smiling country, where hills, woods, fertile fields, and the winding stream of the Susquehanna expressed the beauty and friendliness of nature with nothing of its savagery. These gracious influences became a rich endowment. Nature did for her what it did for Wordsworth's Lucy, imparted to her its mystery, its poise, its solitude, its rhythmic change, its freedom from haste and affectation. Social being as she afterwards became, her days with dumb things were fortunately preparatory. They taught her to know the elemental background of human existence, to respect it, to value in herself and others the blind motions of its unconscious wisdom, and to carry into subsequent life and literature the senses it had trained. She used to pity persons born in cities, and thought that the country-bred were provided with securer sources of happiness. Throughout life, when she would chase fatigue and fear, she fled from "the great town's harsh heart-wearying roar" and quickly renewed herself by lying in green grass or walking by the bank of a favorite brook in the deep woods. There she needed no other companion than the hopping birds. With them she was an intimate from her earliest years, and she became in later life an expert in their names and ways. One of her most successful addresses was on the glories of a country life; and I remember her saying that the opening sections of Emerson's Essay on Nature affected her as if they were the recollections of her brooding childhood. Her refinement had ever an earthy stock beneath it, so that she was not easily shocked or inclined to count common things unclean. She loved to mix with horses. She knew the farmyard, the country road, the breeding cattle, and the upturned soil; and she cared for them as heartily as for college girls, picture galleries, and companies where there are "quick returns of courtesy and wit." When Ulysses stepped naked from the thicket on the seashore, Nausicaä's maidens fled, while she herself stood unalarmed to learn what he might need. Alice Freeman's country training enabled her all her days to behave as did the Phæacian princess.

But persons were with the child as well as natural objects. We are all offshoots of a family. Sometimes we speak as if each of us were a single individual, standing solitary, existing alone; but nothing of the sort is true. The smallest conceivable personality is threefold, — father, mother, child. No one of us starts as an individual or can ever after become such, being essentially social, a member merely, a part of a larger whole. It is therefore of extreme consequence, if our life is to be a fortunate one, that the family of which we are portions shall be noble and have a high descent. That was the case with Alice Freeman; for though on both sides, so far as I am aware, few of her ancestors figured in the newspapers, or had any considerable share of wealth or learning, they were of that sturdy stock which has been the glory of America — men and women who in quiet homes pride themselves on duty and intelligence, who think about each day's work and carefully accomplish it; people on whom neighbors can rely, and who are willing to be overlooked in the public interest. James Warren Freeman, the hard-working, self-forgetting father, was of Scottish blood. His mother was a Knox; her father being James Knox of Washington's Life Guard. From her father

Alice derived much of her moral beauty, and also that gleam of red which undershot her dark hair. Perhaps too from his side came some of her love of adventure; for her paternal grandfather walked from Connecticut through the wilderness and became one of the first settlers of Central New York.

The mother, Elizabeth Josephine Higley — her mother Elvira Frost — was one of five beautiful daughters of a Colesville farmer. Their dark hair and large eyes passed over to the child, their vivacity too, and their forceful intellectual disposition. Mother and grandmother had been for brief terms teachers. The mother herself had unusual executive ability and a strong disposition to improve social conditions around her. She interested herself in temperance, and in legislation for the better protection of women and children. In later years, after a long illness had led her to reflect on the lack of medical provision for women, she raised by her own efforts, though far from rich herself, sufficient money to build and equip an extensive hospital for women in her city of Saginaw. Both father and mother were of large physical frame, tough in fibre, and capable of enduring constant toil. But on the mother's side there was a tendency to consumption.

When Alice was born, her mother was but seventeen and a half years old. "I grew up with my mother," she used to say. In the next five years came a boy and two girls. Neither Mrs. Freeman nor her husband had inherited property, and the conditions of farming in a young country are severe. I remember Alice's speaking of the rarity of fresh meat in her childhood, and of associations of luxury with a keg of salt mackerel. On these isolated farms no servants were kept, nor were means of communication easy. Newspapers, letters, and books were rare. The family itself was the community. Comforts were little thought of. He was lucky who could command the necessities.

It is now acknowledged that the most questionable advantage of large wealth is its influence on children. Those who acquire it are likely enough to grow with its pursuit, and the control over the world which it brings to its vigorous accumulator is not unfavorable to enjoyment or to still further advance. But children who have never known want get few deep draughts of joy. Whoever prizes human conditions in proportion to their tendency to develop powers must commiserate the children of the rich and think of them as our unfortunate classes. They associate less with their parents than do others; their goings and comings are more hampered; they are not so easily habituated to regular tasks; they are pressed less to experiment, foresee, adapt; they have less stimulus to energetic excellence, and when tempted to vice or mediocrity they have little counter-compulsion to support their better purpose. Wise rich parents know these dangers and give their most anxious thought to shielding their children from the enervating influence of wealth.

At the opposite extreme, poverty is for certain children, and at certain ages, tonic in its effect. It may be too severe and become blighting. Middle conditions are for the average undoubtedly safest. At the time of turning from childhood to youth there appears in the normal child a craving for the expansion of personal tastes. If this cannot in some measure be gratified, damage results. The child is stunted. At an earlier age the importance of money is less clear. The child's nature determines whether narrow means are to be a blessing or a curse. A gentle child, slow, unobservant, unromantic, little disposed to projecting itself into things, is in danger of being crushed by a bleak environment, or at least of having its undesirable qualities confirmed. It grows up dull, coarse, or bitter. But little children of a more aggressive type are nourished by poverty and in it are often afforded their best opportunity for early expansion.

So it was with small Alice Freeman. She found a careful home fortunate, or possibly made it so; for in her case the distinction between finding and making was seldom quite clear. She has often assured me of the happiness of her childhood; and one can see how to so rich a nature — alert, forceful, and creative — the exactitudes of a restricted existence might not be unfriendly. In that environment the fourfold germs of the moral sense very early gathered their proper warmth, and grew delightedly toward God, and toward her superiors, inferiors, and equals.

In this home God was reverenced and man content. Both parents were profoundly religious, the father an elder of the Presbyterian church. Whatever came therefore, gentle or severe, was felt to come with kindness and to bring its call to cheerful and considered acceptance. In such serious circumstances the words of the Bible, of the Pilgrim's Progress, of the great hymns, penetrate the soul with a depth of meaning incredible to those who read them carelessly or in the intervals of other exciting volumes. Religion roots best in isolation. "Be still, and know that I am God," says the Psalmist. In the silence of the country a child can hear God's voice. Then too, whatever the hardships were or however severe, they were shared; and difficulties met together strengthened the dearest of human ties. To her young mother Alice soon became rather a sister than a child, a peculiar relation maintained through life, and more natural at that time because there was usually in the house an aunt or two of about her own years.

Where too there was so little money and so much to do, the smallest took part in the universal work; no burdensome part, but one which, though a kind of play, contributed to the common gain. Sociologists say that the sports of animals and children are educative, really performances in miniature and for pure pleasure, of the employments of later life. This buoyant child found participation in the daily toil such an anticipatory sport, and almost from infancy helpfulness grew habitual. About as soon as she could walk she was employed to call her father from the field, to assist her mother with the dishes and the beds, and to gather eggs from the barn. When she was five, she had three younger children to attend, henceforth her daily charge. She dressed them, brushed their hair, took them to school, and performed all those offices of the little mother which fall upon the eldest girl in a household of slender means. These are the kindergartens of the country, admirable training schools for such small persons as can meet their requirements. At an age when children of the well-to-do are hardly out of their nurses' arms Alice Freeman was already well started in heartfelt dependence on the Eternal, in the cheerful performance of regular work, in lightening the labor of those above her, and in accepting responsibility for those below. Any one can see how these early habits prepared her for future power.

Intellectually her case seems less favorable. A district school, of the disordered and elementary sort usual in a sparsely settled country, was the only one accessible. Its teacher was paid two dollars a week and "boarded round." To it Alice went when she was four. But already at three she had taught herself to read, and her beautiful voice was always afterwards much in request for reading aloud — excellent preparation for subsequent public speaking. Though books were few, they were read many times, about the only mode of reading which yields profit to the young. Favorite poems were committed to memory. Alice's first public appearance, occasioned by one of these, amusingly illustrates her instinctive identification of herself with those around.

When five years old she was taken to a village gathering, where the entertainment chiefly consisted of music and speeches. While these incomprehensible matters were in progress she was allowed to fall asleep, but at the appropriate moment was waked, stood on a table, and told to repeat her poem. It was one she was fond of, and she spoke it with the same fervor as if she were alone. The delighted audience broke into applause. But their feelings at once became hers too, and she clapped her little hands as heartily as did any of her hearers. Her parents from the beginning knew her to be a golden child and gave much care to her mental growth.

To it the country also brought its precious contributions. The natural thoughts of a child, the poet says, "are long, long thoughts." Thoughts of these dimensions come most easily in the country. A daguerreotype of her, taken when she was five and published here, shows that she already has them.

Then too while country life, especially in the early years, benumbs the intellect that is merely scholastic, it calls into perpetual activity the practical intellect in those fortunate enough to possess it. In the country, when one needs anything, he cannot step into a neighboring store and purchase for his use what has been provided by the forethought of others. He is dependent on himself. He must find, invent, or go without his article; either master nature or be mastered by her. It is true that in the long run the majority of country people are mastered and tamely submit to daily inconvenience. Nevertheless it is a great advantage to a vigorous young person, destined for future affairs, to be brought up where there is little division of labor, where therefore ready wits and practical good sense are at a constant premium. On the whole we must count Alice Freeman fortunate in those early circumstances which shaped her originally strong intelligence and fitted it for diverse and ready action.

But there is one danger which besets so restricted a household. However intelligent, industrious, or

Portrait at five years

brave, it tends to routine and to resting satisfied with the supply of daily needs. Ideals die under too great pressure. But that was not the case here; for hers were ambitious parents, ambitious for attaining wider work through self-improvement. The father was a man of unusual kindness, much disposed to look after those about him. By degrees the idea of becoming a physician took strong hold of him. It was encouraged by his wife, who offered to maintain herself and the four children during the two years' absence necessary for his training at the Albany Medical School. And this was actually accomplished between Alice's seventh and ninth years. Where means were found for maintaining father and family during the audacious interval I have never been able to discover. Of course the cares of the household were doubled, yet in so splendid a cause as to fix forever in the mind of one of them the wisdom of sacrificing present comforts to ideal ends. Alice Freeman never forgot those glorious years. They were among the few events of her childhood to which she often referred; for they set a pattern to which she was ever after eager to conform, of noble aims, willing suffering, resourcefulness, persistence, and ultimate arrival at greater ability to serve.

When Dr. Freeman returned, equipped for professional work, a change of residence became advisable. The farm was abandoned and a house was taken in the village of Windsor. Practice came quickly to one who was as truly a physician of the mind and soul as of the body. Soon it extended over miles of the surrounding country. In his long rides among his scattered patients a little girl accompanied her father. To drive was exhilarating; she talked to him on the road; she held the horse during his visit; and when he came forth grave from the bedside, she shared his anxieties over the dangerous case. So the intimacy between the pair grew strong. Among her papers written in later life I find a passage evidently suggested by these early years in which she uses their happy memories to interpret similar experiences in the life of a friend who had died. Of this friend she writes: —

"She was fortunate in being bred in the country, responsive to its birds and flowers, to the stars above her head and the stones under her feet, and to the simplicity of its quiet pleasures. A country doctor's granddaughter, she came close in childhood to his good and high influence, close to sickness, to sorrow, to hardship, and to loss. In sympathetic relations with him she learned to love humankind in all degrees of trouble and poverty, as well as to rejoice in natural beauty. She has told me of that village home and her village friends. We who knew her used often to say, even down to these last years, 'You have a girl's heart and a country girl's loves and enthusiasms.' It made no difference that she went forth into high public station. She brought back from the drawing-rooms of Washington and the salons of Paris the highmindedness, the human affections, and the swift sympathies which her grandfather gave her through long contact with sorrow and heart-break."

It would be hard to describe more exactly what Alice Freeman derived from her father, and perhaps it may be well to show here the permanence of that influence, and the sort of passionate devotion it fixed in her for the silent man who gave it. I quote some lines which she wrote the year before she died. Dr. Freeman had been struck down by a violent illness which seemed likely to bring sudden death. She was summoned from Cambridge by telegraph. As she rode she wrote the following verses, showing them to no one. After her death I found them among her papers, marked "On the Train, April 12, 1902." The reference in the fifth stanza is to her sister Stella, who had died twenty-three years before.

How long and weary stretch the miles away
  Between us, O my father, as I come
To catch again your dear voice, if I may,
  Here in our earthly home.

Perhaps ere this your lips are cold and still;
  Perhaps you hear the angels' triumph song,

And smile upon us from some heavenly hill
  The blessed saints among.

They are not sick or sorry any more;
  And you are strong and young and glad again.
What will you do on that wide shining shore
  Where all are free from pain?

All your long life you healed the sick and sad;
  You gave as God gives, counting not the cost.
Your presence made the little children glad;
  With you no soul was lost.

How many happy ones will greet you there
  About our starlike girl, so long away!
Ah, but to see her shining eyes and hair
  As on that sad June day!

I will not grieve, my father, for your peace.
  I will rejoice if you have won your rest
Where Springs fade not, where sorrows ever cease,
  And all the good are blest.

III

GIRLHOOD

The settlement at Windsor marks a second period in Alice Freeman's life. By degrees she turns from childhood to girlhood. What the nature of the change is, or at what precise time it occurs, is seldom evident either to onlookers or to the child herself. But the transition, though gradual, is momentous and not altogether pleasing. In Alice Freeman I judge it appeared about two years earlier than ordinary.

Girlhood begins when little by little the child comes to think for herself and to regard herself as a person of importance. She accordingly seeks to assert and enlarge that importance. Earlier than this she has hardly had possession of her powers. By herself and others she has been accounted merely a member of a family. Few articles are called hers. Her wishes are not much regarded. She is included in family plans, but has too little experience and foresight to form them. Very properly she is expected to subordinate herself to her elders, the chief work of the years of childhood being to train us to live in collective fashion. We then accept the property, knowledge, beliefs, habits, ideals accumulated in the family group. During absorptive childhood we have little which we have not received.

Maturity discloses more. Gradually we become aware of something precious within us which is just ourself. We are somebody. The consciousness that I am I parts me from others. Not that we then cease to recognize duties to the family. These continue, but undergo a change. Henceforth we perform them in freedom, conscious that we too are persons of importance and have duties to ourselves as well. Other people are now discovered to be "selves" also, and the adjustment of us to them becomes a puzzling problem. The period when this self-consciousness begins to make itself felt is usually an awkward one. The early spontaneous charm has disappeared, while personal dignity has not yet arisen. Jarrings and antagonisms are ordinary indications that such a period is approaching.

That one so sympathetic as Alice Freeman would be saved from the worst of such clashes may easily be guessed. I can learn of few of the self-assertions and aberrations which usually appear in this epoch-making transition. She had a will of her own, was liable to anger, and easily resented personal annoyance. But her consciousness of much beside herself steadied her. Even in parting from the family she took the family with her. Once at evening prayers a large June-bug buzzed through the window and

THE SUSQUEHANNA VALLEY
as seen from the Freeman House, Windsor, New York

settled in a curl of her hair. He would not be detached. She kept herself quiet through the several minutes of prayer; then, as all rose from their knees, she cried out, "I wanted to scream, but I could n't upset you and God." "Of course not," said her father, gravely dislodging the creature. For a good while bursts of passion broke out when her will was crossed. She would throw herself down and beat the floor with her heels. But when one day she saw her brother in a similar paroxysm, she examined him with horror and at bedtime told her mother that she should never be angry again. "Fred must n't be." And though through after life rage at wrong often boiled below the surface and came to an occasional explosion, it was soon controlled, and rarely parted her from him who occasioned it.

Yet however considerately the transition was managed, childhood, the period of absorption in the family, was ending as Alice Freeman settled into the new life at Windsor; self-seeking girlhood began, an epoch stretching forward as far as the attainment of the college degree. In this period the vigorous girl or boy longs for enlargement, the forces ordinarily impelling most powerfully toward it being education, love, and religion. All these came to Alice Freeman, as they come to every girl; but to her they came unusually early, orderly, and transformingly.

The considerable village of Windsor where the family was now living contained a school of superior rank, Windsor Academy. Its principal, Joseph Eastman, was a man of more breadth than most country towns can show. After graduating from Dartmouth, he had gone through the Harvard Medical School and Andover Theological Seminary. He was now both minister of the Presbyterian Church in the village and principal of the Academy. Besides himself the Academy employed half a dozen other teachers, gave instruction in the languages, and was the finishing school for most of its students. It was much like one of our modern high schools, though of looser organization and without the dominant aim of preparing its pupils for college. On coming to Windsor Dr. Freeman did much to raise its grade and to change it from the school of a village to an academy for all the country around. This school Alice entered in September, 1865. Here her real education began. Previously she had been her own teacher, or had picked up what little was to be had on the benches of a district school. Here at the age of ten she learned to mix with a considerable company of girls and boys, to feel the influence of accomplished teachers, to see how large is the field of knowledge and how small the amount which any one can gather. Young as she was, she eagerly seized her opportunity and began to form interests of her own. Throughout life she acknowledged her indebtedness to this important school; and when in 1901 the Academy celebrated its semi-centennial, she visited it and renewed her gratitude to it and its pretty village. From a report of her address on that occasion I take the following passage: —

"Words do not tell what this old school and place meant to me as a girl. I am proud to say that I was the daughter of a farmer of the Susquehanna, and for me there never can be another such village as this. When I graduated in 1872 and went a thousand miles westward to college, I bore away remembrances of our magnificent river, its enormous width, strong currents, and terrible freshets. But I recall that when a college classmate came home with me for a vacation, her eyes were reproachful as she said, 'I thought you told me it was larger than the Mississippi.' I believed then that all the nicest people lived in Windsor; that all the patriots of the country were of our political party — no matter which party; and that all the good people belonged to the Presbyterian Church. No one told me so, but I believed it. I have changed my mind about some things since then. But my faith in the old school has not grown less, but more. Here we gathered abundant Greek, Latin, French and Mathematics, though we have forgotten a part; here we were taught truthfulness, to be upright and honorable; here we had our first loves, our first hopes, our first ambitions, our first dreams, and some of us our first disappointments. We owe a large debt to Windsor Academy for the solid groundwork of education which it laid." I still have her little Greek Testament with the name of the Academy penciled on the fly-leaf.

That from the first she was something of a leader in the school I infer from the following anecdote. In the winter of 1867, when she was twelve, four schools of Broome County held a literary contest. Each school was to prepare a set of compositions. These were to be put in charge of a delegate for arrangement and for public reading. The other schools chose teachers as delegates; Windsor chose her. She carried off the prize on all three counts: for arrangement, for reading, and for her own composition.

In 1868 a deeper impulse began. There came to the Academy a singularly inspiring teacher. Such an event has formed the turning-point of many a life, and more often than any other has been decisive in bringing about a studious career. Some one person has vitalized knowledge for us — it matters little what branch — and almost magically our vague and variable desires for learning, power, public service, become crystallized and take a shape which defies the batterings of after years. Personal influence is a commanding factor everywhere; but nowhere has it so immediate or lasting an effect as in the schools.

Alice's teacher was a young man who, after graduating from Union College, had spent a year in Princeton Theological Seminary. Being in debt for his college education, he thought it well before advancing further toward his profession to teach a while at Windsor. There he deeply influenced the whole school, for his character was as strong as his scholarship. But he had the discernment to single out a child in one of the lower classes, and to this large-eyed girl gave special care. Apparently from the first he knew her precocious ability. Whether she would ever have known it if he had not given her insight, I have doubted. He taught her both accuracy and enthusiasm. He made her think herself worth while. He lent her books, fashioned her tastes, talked with her, walked with her, showed her a great human being to admire, made clearer her reverence for Nature and for God, and in the two years of their acquaintance transformed her into a woman. Was it strange that he then began to love her whom he had seemed to create? I have told how she was always long in advance of her years. His sure eye knew incipient excellence, and his idealizing nature enjoyed beauty before it was blown. One gets a high impression of a man who could be so affected by an unfolding thing. On her side there seems to have been dumb wonder and obedient esteem. How could she refuse what one so exalted asked? She could comprehend little of his love. Through all he had done for her she had more easily felt a great influence than understood its words. But if in that high region where he lived he wished her company, her merry laughter, her picture, her hand, who else could have an equal right? With few girlish dreams and small foresight of the future, but seriously and with dignity, she consented to an engagement at fourteen.

In every deep nature thoughts of love are allied with thoughts of God. This year she joined the Presbyterian Church. It is a heroic moment for any one of us when, face to face with God, we formally announce that henceforth we are accountable to Him alone. It marks the attainment of full self-consciousness. The young soul now takes itself in charge and says, "Mine is the decision. I have chosen my way of laying hold on life." The authority of parents is at an end, supplanted by the laws of reason, righteousness, and human welfare. So at least Alice Freeman understood her crisis. To it education, love, and religion all contributed. Experiences which fall upon most of us separately and at much later periods she encountered in their collective force when she had barely entered her teens. Her scale of growth is different from the ordinary. She needed to start early, so as to pack into her forty-seven years what others hardly include in their threescore and ten.

Always devout, she now consecrated herself, and for the rest of her life the desire for the utmost service of God's children seems to inspire every private impulse. In her case religion did not appear in its negative character, as restraint; it always signified joyous freedom and enlargement. It brought assurance of humanity's kinship with the power which dominates all. No situation can therefore arise in which hostile forces are engaged against us, nor need we be crushed by an indifferent world. Every harshest circumstance contains some novel mode of access to God and our broader life. Of these matters she seldom spoke. I never knew her to argue them. They merely represent her working conviction, confirmed by every day's experience. Thus she viewed things, and things were ever ready to respond. Most of us lightly assume as an ultimate ground of all some sort of blind force, incomprehensible stuff which we should be incapable of demonstrating if challenged. She thought personal life as she knew it in herself more intelligible, particularly as it rendered an otherwise stupid world intelligible too, and enabled her everywhere to live in her Father's house.

But the broader outlook on life now gained was not altogether favorable to her engagement. Her lover had let loose forces which soon passed beyond his control. He had revealed her worth, a worth which involved responsibility for its care. He had opened unsuspected capacities which must now be filled. Through him, the first college graduate she had known, she discovered what the higher training signifies. She was to be a fellow-worker with God. To make herself as efficient as possible became then the most urgent of duties. These were the thoughts which gradually took shape in her puzzled mind during the years 1869–71. For the paths of culture and allegiance soon divided. In 1870 he was to enter Yale Theological Seminary and make his final preparation for the ministry. He proposed that she should spend this time in completing her course at Windsor, and afterwards join him in some country parish. The proposal revealed what marriage with him would mean. In it she would give but half herself. Such a fictitious union would dishonor both him and her. She was too young, too unexpanded. Until she had undergone college discipline she would not have matured herself sufficiently to deserve a strong man's love. Marriage, as she now and henceforth conceived it, was to be a comradeship of equals where each contributes rich powers of different kinds to a mutual life.

Accordingly six months after he had left her for New Haven they parted, parted with kindness and deep respect. He no less than she approved the separation. I believe they never met again. After two years in Yale Seminary he became a minister, and until his death was loved by all who knew him. He married, and had a daughter whom he named Alice. Neither could ever have regretted any part of the invigorating connection. She has repeatedly spoken to me of her debt to him who first awakened her, to him who accompanied her so delicately through difficult paths of decision, and who was in himself so admirable.

Nor did his chivalrous protection of her cease with his departure. In his company she had learned once for all what she desired in marriage, and she was henceforth guarded against casual and unworthy impulses as few young women are. It was often thought strange that one of such beauty, responsiveness, and social opportunity could so long remain single. In all other experiences of life she anticipated her sex. Was this delay due to disparagement of marriage? No, but to the very reverse. And because I perceive how impossible it is to make her career comprehensible if I conceal these intimate facts, I here set down a simple statement of them.

One set of difficulties in the way of going to college was now removed. Another remained. Her parents opposed the plan. Few had ever gone to college from those parts, nor was it usual for girls to go at all. The family means were scanty, though slightly improved since farming days. The younger children were becoming expensive. Dr. Freeman told his daughter that it would be impossible for more than one of the children to be given a college education, and that this one ought to be the son, as he must ultimately support the family. Alice declared that she meant to have a college degree if it took her till she was fifty to get it. If her parents could help her, even partially, she would promise never to marry until she had herself put her brother through college and given to each of her sisters whatever education they might wish — a promise subsequently performed. She pointed out the importance to all the family of her becoming one of its supports instead of one of its dependents. The discussions were long and grave, but her judgment finally prevailed. She was to graduate from the Academy at seventeen, and it was agreed that she should then immediately enter college.

In the year before she went two events occurred deserving mention. The Windsor church found that its evening meetings were unattractive on account of inadequate light. There was no central chandelier, and the few lamps scattered about the room left it cheerless. Though Alice was then gathering means for her college course, she presented a chandelier to the church, earning the money that winter and going without a coat.

During the winter, too, Anna Dickinson came to Binghamton for an evening lecture on Joan of Arc. Alice had never heard a woman speak. She persuaded her father to take her in the sleigh over the more than twenty miles of dark country road, and was deeply moved by the speaker.

In deciding on a college the range of choice was small. Wellesley, Smith, and Bryn Mawr were not yet in existence. Mount Holyoke was still a "Female Seminary," and Elmira hardly more, though legally a college. To this latter she might naturally have gone, as the college for girls nearest at hand. But she had been reading college catalogues, and knew that Elmira standards were low. To Vassar, which had just been founded, she seems to have inclined for a moment. But was it a true college, or merely another Elmira? A boy in her class who was preparing for Amherst hinted that these girls' colleges were a contrivance for enabling women to pretend that they had the same education as men. She had suspected as much herself, and, being determined to get the best, had already begun to turn toward coeducation. But coeducational colleges were at that time few. Michigan was the strongest of them, and had opened its doors to women only two years before. That, then, distant though it was, she chose.

IV

THE UNIVERSITY

In June, 1872, Dr. Freeman took his daughter to Ann Arbor to see the University, attend Commencement, and pass the entrance examinations. But here her resolution met with a sharp rebuff. She failed. Good as the Academy had been for supplying general knowledge, it was poorly equipped for preparing pupils for college. The failure, however, proved as fortunate as everything else which befell this favored girl, for it brought her to the notice of the remarkable man who from that day took her under his peculiar charge. President Angell himself shall tell the story: —

"In 1872, when Alice Freeman presented herself at my office, accompanied by her father, to apply for admission to the University, she was a simple, modest girl of seventeen. She had pursued her studies in the little Academy at Windsor. Her teachers regarded her as a child of much promise, precocious, possessed of a bright, alert mind, of great industry, of quick sympathies, and of an instinctive desire to be helpful to others. Her preparation for college had been meagre, and both she and her father were

UNIVERSITY HALL, MICHIGAN UNIVERSITY

doubtful of her ability to pass the required examinations. The doubts were not without foundation. The examiners, on inspecting her work, were inclined to decide that she ought to do more preparatory work before they could accept her. Meantime I had had not a little conversation with her and her father, and had been impressed with her high intelligence. At my request the examiners decided to allow her to enter on a trial of six weeks. I was confident she would demonstrate her capacity to go on with her class. I need hardly add that it was soon apparent to her instructors that my confidence was fully justified. She speedily gained and constantly held an excellent position as a scholar."

But the deficiencies of the past hampered progress. Already she was much in need of rest after the strain of preparation; yet all the summer before entrance had to be spent in clearing away conditions, and she remained in Ann Arbor through the vacations of that year, engaged in study for the same purpose. This business of removing conditions went on, too, side by side with the regular college work, lowering the grade of the latter and causing frequent exhaustion. At intervals the assistance of a teacher became necessary, still further depleting her scanty means. Throughout her college course solicitudes over time, health, and money never ceased. Yet anxieties seem rather to have caused elation over what was already had than depression over what might be missed. College training had been so long desired that it was welcomed now on any terms.

And indeed on almost any terms it is delightful. For most of us the period of learning is a period of romance. We are young, and all things are possible. Every circumstance is novel, calculated in some way to serve our growth and happiness. Even those of us who have spent our early years in toil learn at last how to profit by play. We make a few intimate friends and a wide circle of acquaintances. We fashion our ideals, compare them with those about us, and have them sharply criticised. The physical world more deeply discloses its wonders. Through many avenues we enter into the heritage of the race. Whatever is precious in the past and has been thought worth preserving in the caskets called books is offered for our enrichment. And in our teachers we have wise guides who not only conduct us to these treasures, but point out their human significance. It must be an abnormal girl or boy who does not count such years happy.

All this Miss Freeman felt. To her the absurdly named town of Ann Arbor was ever afterwards sacred soil. She visited it as often as possible, and everywhere her face brightened at the sight of a classmate. Notwithstanding many disturbances, she has repeatedly told me of the extreme pleasure and profit of these years; and in her little book, "Why Go to College," she has given a glowing picture of the gain which the experiences of college bring to every earnest girl. I regret therefore that most of her college letters, being chiefly of a business nature, imperfectly express her gaiety or even her studious interests. From them, however, aided by the recollection of classmates, I am able to present a tolerable account of her intellectual, social, religious, physical, and financial progress during these college years.

Her scholarly work cannot, I suppose, be called quite solid. There was too much of it for that. The regular studies were abundant; the addition of those which should have been ended in the preparatory school made the amount burdensome; and this became overwhelming when increased by the worthy engagements outside study which in this place of opportunity solicited a hitherto secluded girl. From intellectual disaster she was saved by a peculiarity of her constitution. To an astonishing degree she was always swiftly absorptive. Whatever in her neighborhood contained human nutriment was perceived and seized at once. All became hers with slight expenditure of time or effort. Throughout life she gathered half-instinctively an amount of knowledge which others obtain only by toil. A mother whose son was in the University at this time relates how he used to come home saying, "There's a girl in my class who knows everything — everything!" And one who was associated with her in the teaching of history at Wellesley tells me that she herself rarely gained any new historic insight and reported it to Miss Freeman without finding that Miss Freeman was familiar with it already. Indeed her sympathy with truth was so broad and discerning that reality opened itself to her on every side. Could she have had more leisure at the University, she might have distinguished herself there; though perhaps even then her liking for every species of knowledge would have prevented eminence. She would not concentrate attention on certain subjects to the neglect of others. Such specialization was less the habit of her day than of ours. So she was free to approach all, and in all she managed to obtain a good rank. History, Greek, English literature, and to some extent mathematics, were the studies that left the deepest impression; chiefly, I suspect, because of the excellence of the instruction in these subjects.

Her memory was good and her observation accurate. I think she retained more of what she learned than is common. One is often struck with the small stock of knowledge carried off from study, even by those who obtain through it decided intellectual advantage. Maturing influences and facts acquired seem to have little relation; and no doubt if one of these is to be lost, the detailed truths had better go. Miss Freeman kept a good balance between the contrasted gains. During these years her mind grew rapidly in range, subtlety, coherence, and in persistent power of work. But she bore away also a body of knowledge which served her well in her career as a teacher and in the subsequent varied demands of a busy life. At Commencement a part was assigned her, one of the first granted to the girl students of Michigan. President Angell tells me it captured the attention of her audience and held it firmly throughout. Its subject was "The Relations of Science and Poetry" — an indication, I suppose, that she had already come upon some of the fundamental problems which vex the scholar's mind.

But of at least equal importance with the knowledge acquired in college is the influence on a student of the personality of his teachers. Some of these, it is true, will always be mere purveyors of knowledge; others, more insignificant still, inspectors of what has been learned already. But in every college faculty there are pretty sure to be certain men of mark, from whom — sometimes in the course of instruction, sometimes through personal acquaintance — a student half-imperceptibly carries off impressions and impulses of incalculable worth. In such weighty personalities the University of Michigan in Miss Freeman's time was exceptionally rich. Half a dozen of them helped to shape this responsive girl.

Of familiar intercourse with her teachers I suspect she enjoyed more than is generally obtainable to-day. President and Mrs. Angell had her much in their beautiful home, as did in different degrees Professors D'Ooge, Tyler, and Adams. These men enriched her outside the classroom and became her lifelong friends. While she was in college they watched over her carefully, and when she went forth they opened before her the difficult doors of the world.

In those days women's education was an anxious experiment. At graduation her class contained sixty-four men and eleven women. The girls were therefore studied by others and themselves a little unduly. Heartily welcomed everywhere though they were, they could not take what each day brought quite as a matter of course. Being pioneers and representatives of many who would come afterwards, they were burdened with a sense of responsibility. According as they conducted themselves their sisters would have ampler or narrower opportunities. Such conscious conditions insure uprightness, but are hardly so favorable for ease and the graces. They had at least the good effect of banding the girls together and uniting the little group by something like a family tie. Though Miss Freeman was one of the younger members of this family, she quickly became its head by virtue of her practical sagacity, moral force, and personal attractiveness. President Angell writes: —

"One of her most striking characteristics in college was her warm and demonstrative sympathy with her circle of friends. Her soul seemed bubbling over with joy, which she wished to share with the other girls. While she was therefore in the most friendly relations with all the girls then in college, she was the radiant centre of a considerable group whose tastes were congenial with her own. Without assuming or striving for leadership, she could not but be to a certain degree a leader among these, some of whom have since attained positions only less conspicuous for usefulness than her own. Her nature was so large and generous, so free from envy, that she was esteemed by all her comrades, whether they cherished exactly her ideals or not. Wherever she went, her genial outgoing spirit seemed to carry with her an atmosphere of cheerfulness and joy. No girl of her time on withdrawing from college would have been more missed than she."

She joined several college clubs, distinguished herself in the debating society, was fond of long walks through the fertile Michigan country, and always had leisure for a share in whatever picnic, sleighride, or student entertainment called for merriment, adventure, inventiveness, or social tact.

Throughout life she thought herself fortunate in having chosen a coeducational college. The natural association of girls with boys in interests of a noble sort tends, she believed, to broaden their vision, to solidify their minds, and to remove much that is hectic and unwholesome from the awakening instincts of sex. She did not think it made girls boyish, or boys girlish; but merely that it brought good sense and a pleased companionship to take the place of giddiness and sentimentality. She used to say that co-educational marriages seldom appear in the divorce courts. I think her own manners — as quiet and free among men as among women — owed much of their naturalness to the fact that at no period of her life did men become strange. Professor Hale of Chicago has well said, "It was Mrs. Palmer's conviction that the normal form of education for both sexes is that in which the natural relations — begun in the life of the home and the neighborhood, continued for the great majority in the life of the school, and inevitably existing in the later social life — are carried without break through the four years of higher intellectual work. She may have been right or she may have been wrong; but that such a woman, with her personal experience of Ann Arbor, of Wellesley, of Radcliffe, and of Harvard, should have held this belief is a fact to be reckoned with." In tracing her development at Ann Arbor we must not omit to notice the ability she gained there to comprehend a man's world. Certainly from that university came many of the best ideals of college structure which subsequently entered into the foundation of Wellesley. I doubt if she could have built that woman's college so strongly if she had not herself been trained in the company of men.

Side by side with the studious and social interests of college life went religion, of which they were in reality only a special expression; for religion glorified her entire existence. One who knew her well at this time says that even then "her religious life was of that cheerful, inspiring type which characterized it in her maturer years and which always commended the Christian faith in winsome ways to those who came within her influence."

At the beginning of her residence in Ann Arbor she connected herself with the Presbyterian Church, of which Samuel Willoughby Duffield was the pastor. He was a man of enthusiasm and scholarship, in many respects akin to herself, and to him she became warmly attached. Every Sunday she attended two church services, taught in the Sunday School, in a mission school also, and was usually present at one or two services during the week. But into the College Christian Association she threw herself with the utmost ardor, vitalizing that body and delivering it from the narrowness which in those days often beset such organizations. She brought it to represent more than a single type of character. While she was its leader it became a strong power for righteousness throughout the entire town. To her, too, her classmates, men and women, most naturally turned as a spiritual adviser. The knowledge she thus obtained of the troubles of the young, real or imaginary, proved useful in the larger contacts of later years, and even now began to shape the ideals of what she meant to do. Before she left college, the desire to deepen, to lighten, to render more intelligent and joyous the lives of girls and women, had become clearly defined.

I have said that consumption was in her family, and that from childhood she had never been strong. The lungs and heart were weak and there was a disposition to colds and fatigue. That "outgoing spirit" too, of which President Angell speaks, continually exposed her to excessive strain. Whatever human interest or need appeared in her neighborhood was pretty sure to receive attention. To consider and spare herself never became instinctive, though in later years she trained her powers to some degree of restraint for the sake of broader use. But swift responsiveness and a kind of spendthrift generosity have ever been beautiful faults of admirable women. Even Providence seems unfairly indulgent to self-forgetting souls and unaccountably wards off from them appropriate harm. How she accomplished all she did, accomplished it too with distinction, is a mystery. On account of an interruption in her junior year, she had as a senior twenty hours a week of recitations, and no less as a freshman, though her social and religious engagements were alone sufficient to fill her time. Yet she graduated, as do most girls, stronger than she entered. Studying is wholesome business; and after all, college life has more regular hours and more invigorating agencies than most homes can offer. But considering her inheritance, the exhausting nature of the last two years at Windsor, and the burden of her deficient preparation, it is not strange that her letters often speak of being "tired" and of the hope that her cold "will be better next week." One of the professors whom she saw oftenest tells me he frequently remonstrated with her over the cough she brought to college, a cough which continued until a few years before her death.

Financial anxieties burdened her too. There was always uncertainty whether she would be able to continue in college another year. From the beginning her parents had strained their slender purse to the utmost, and she herself earned whatever was possible. But resources still remained small and expenses large. To bring the two at all together called for restraint, courage, ingenuity, and a readiness to do things for herself. I have thought it well to print one or two letters which show the details of this pathetic struggle. They can hardly be read without tears and smiles. But every college teacher will recognize them as typical letters, such as still go home from every part of the country where brave young men and women are using skill and dignity to compass knowledge.

The circumstances of the family had not improved. When Miss Freeman entered college, prospects were bright. Considerable woodlands on the farm promised, if properly developed, to yield a good return; but such development required money and constant supervision, while a country doctor could furnish little of either. In consequence, each year grew harder than the one before. Floods too along the Susquehanna finally swept away a great body of lumber which had gradually been collected there. In the middle of her junior year letters from home disclosed serious entanglement. She did not wait for consultation with her family, but applied at once to President Angell for a position as a teacher, accepted an appointment, travelled to her new home at Ottawa, Illinois, and was already established in her duties there before she informed her parents. This was in January, 1875, when she was not twenty years old.

The Ottawa High School had suddenly lost its principal and needed a prudent management to keep it from going to pieces. She became its head. It was the first school in which she ever taught, while many of its pupils were nearly her own age. The other schools of the town were subordinate to this, and their teachers were men and women of experience. The amount of her teaching, principally in Greek and Latin, was large; and what was not contracted for, though equally necessary, was more difficult still,—the winning of the confidence of her pupils and the town. She gave of her best. At the close of the twenty weeks for which she had engaged herself, she was urged by all connected with the school to remain in it permanently. But she declined. The salary had been ample. Out of it she relieved the family necessities and secured the finishing of her college course. After spending the summer at home she returned to Ann Arbor, making up the omitted studies partly during the vacation and partly in connection with the work of the senior year.

For the brief selection of letters which follows I am fortunate in finding some that picture the ordinary current of college affairs; some that show its perplexities; some that reveal a spirit already moving toward self-confidence and reform; some written at Ottawa, where the first success is had in teaching. I do not date them. It is not always possible. And they are arranged rather by subject than by time. All are youthful, artless, hasty, intended for only the receiver's eye. But surely the lucidity and elevation of their young writer will please.

LETTERS

Dear ones at home, you will expect a letter from me immediately; so, though I am very tired, I am going to write. Read it if you can. I arrived at 50 State Street at noon about an hour ago, and found Mrs. Williams expecting me. I have a pleasant room, nicely furnished, with everything any one could want, even to bookshelves: a pretty little stove, an ingrain carpet, a table and cover. Mrs. Williams had dinner waiting, and I am sure it will be a pleasant boarding-place. On one side of the house there is a large brick building, where there is a school for little children. Just now they are making all the noise it is possible for boys to make. On the other side they are building a church. So this afternoon, when my head aches, my surroundings are not quite perfect; but I think I shall get used to it after a little while.

Coming here I rode in the car where you put me, without changing until just before reaching Niagara Falls. At Elmira a young gentleman and his sister came into my car. They were going West too. He saw I was alone and spoke to me, after which we three went together. The conductor told us if we would exchange for a berth on the sleeper we could go through to Detroit without further change. So the young man took a berth for his sister and myself, and slept on a couch near by. They were bound for Chicago, and took the drawing-room coach at Detroit. We parted company there. It was pleasant for me; but we don't know each other's names, only his sister called him "Joe." He bought us nice grapes at London, with which we stained our dresses. The car from Detroit to Ann Arbor was crowded, but another accommodating young man gave me his seat. All the way I have been fortunate and have had to spend only $2.75. I shall write again very soon.

I have just passed five examinations and feel pretty well satisfied with the result of my semester's work. We had the usual number of visitors and spectators. I was called up for oral examination in everything, but was fortunate enough not to blunder and so can't complain.

In Latin something happened which amused the boys very much. Professor Frieze has just returned from Europe and of course does n't know any of us yet. After we had been writing for some time and all the company had come in, our Professor Walter called up Miss Freeman. He named one of Horace's long hard Satires, giving me a book and asking me to read it, "thinking it would be interesting to the gentlemen." It happened to be one I knew perfectly, and I read it immediately — apparently to the astonishment of Professor Frieze. As I finished, Professor Walter said to him, "Have you any questions?" Professor Frieze looked at me gravely, shook his head, and growled, "No. What's her name?" Then the boys laughed.

In Greek too I could n't have asked a better chance to show off. Professor Pattingill expressed his approbation. This is boasting enough, but I thought you'd want to know how your little girl is prospering. There is an unheard-of number conditioned, over eighty in one class, but only one girl. Our class, too, is noted for its high scholarship. My special studies this semester are Juvenal's Satires, Calculus, and Astronomy, with all of which I am delighted.

I have received all the letters you mention, but have only $16.00. Perhaps you have sent more and I have made some mistake. But I think not. Never mind. I'll pay it all back some time. I ought to settle my account here as soon as possible. If papa can send me money for the bills I shall be very glad. Provisions are very high, as usual in spring, and my bills are still more at the Club.

I have been just as economical as possible all the year, but of course the money you have been able to send has n't been sufficient. We have had to burn a great deal of wood, as it has been and still is very cold; and my bill will be a little over $12.00. I had to get me a new pair of shoes. You know I had only the cloth ones which I wore last summer. They lasted until this spring. I wore my blue hat just as it was all winter, and am wearing my old black one now. I got two yards of black ribbon and trimmed it myself. I bought a pair of cheap black kid gloves a few days ago, some lace for my neck and sleeves, and a fresh ribbon. I have got nothing I could do without; but you know I have to be dressed well all the time in the position I am in. I think I have all the books I shall need. They have cost me more than usual. But the most of the money you have sent has been paid for board.

If you can help me through this year I will try as best I may to take up the paddle and push my own canoe afterwards. Whatever comes, dear mother, I know is best for me. It is all right. Still I believe God helps only those who help themselves. I shall try to do my part, and I fully expect He will do the rest. Mother dear, I have come to several places, even so soon, where I could only see one step ahead; but as soon as I have taken that, another has been opened for me. That is all, I suppose, that is really necessary, though it is n't very pleasant. So I am waiting and trusting and working just as hard as I can while the day lasts. Don't make yourself unhappy nor let any of the rest do so. Why should you when He has said, "Seek first the kingdom of God and *all things* shall be added." If our Father wants me to go through college, I know I shall go; and if He does n't, I don't want to. That is the end of it. Meanwhile I am planning and thinking. If it comes to anything, I will report.

Now I must stop and get a lesson in rhetoric of thirty pages for to-morrow at eight o'clock. You see my life in these days is full. I try to do just as much every day as I would if it were my last in college. It is n't long now before I shall see you, and you will see your tired child.

Ann Arbor has been in uncontrollable excitement this week. Thirty boys have been suspended for the remainder of the year, and one expelled. It is said to be a thing unheard-of in the history of American colleges. I send you only two of the numerous publications on the affair. I never went through such a week in my life. You don't know anything about it unless you are in the midst of it. The senior and junior classes are aroused, and the whole body of students "bolted" chapel two mornings last week. At a great meeting a petition was sent to the Faculty, signed by sixty-five sophomores and seventy freshmen, asking to be sent off too, as they were equally guilty. If there is a general suspension, the two classes will go in a body to Cornell. The boys who did n't sign the petition have promised to go too. It is the greatest shaking which the college has ever had.

Small-pox is spreading dreadfully. It was taken from a subject in the dissecting room, and over thirty of the medical students have it. One died of it yesterday. As soon as cases break out they are taken to the pest-house, though some are too sick to be moved. A panic prevails and the citizens are trying to have the university closed. This certainly will not be done until after examination time, though possibly then if the disease continues to spread. A great many students have gone home, but I'm not afraid. I should be more afraid to set off travelling now.

I went to the Opera last week with Mr. W. I can't describe it to you. It was all light and music and dancing, magnificent costumes and amazing transactions, very brilliant and graceful and beautiful. The house was crowded. I wore my blue suit, which, with my blue and white hat and white gloves, makes a pretty outfit for such an occasion. I enjoyed the evening exceedingly. But I found myself handed to my door at eleven o'clock with a nervous headache and a very tired body. It pays to go once, but it would n't do for a University girl, with her head and hands more than full, to indulge in such exciting pleasures often.

I'm sorry I could n't write you on Sunday, but I was very busy, had my hat off only once between church and bed-time, and that was when I ate my dinner. It was the first Sunday when it has n't rained since I came from home. Church begins at half-past ten. Then comes my Bible class till two. At half-past two I go to the class in the Greek Testament. On Sundays dinner is at three. After it F. and I went over to the cemetery, — as beautiful a place as you can think of — so many trees there, as shady and still as a forest. I never saw so many squirrels, and they say it is full of birds in summer. I could spend a week there. Then the young people of the Presbyterian Church have a prayer-meeting at six o'clock, which I always attend, and preaching comes at seven. Of late there has been great interest in religion here. Our meetings are full.

At my mission school there are about eighty scholars and only six or seven teachers. Several of these attend pretty irregularly. The children are mostly German, bright and interesting. The superintendent is a senior in college. He told me this afternoon that he had given me the worst class in school, but he wanted me to try them. They have had a variety of teachers, who have n't succeeded in keeping even decent order. Some of them are certainly bold and bad looking. They are boys from ten to fifteen and are pretty nearly unmanageable.

Well, it's an experiment, and I suppose they will give me more than one problem this winter. I'm sure I had my hands full this afternoon.

This is the first day of vacation. I have been so busy this year that it seems good to get a change, even though I do keep right on here at work. For some time I have been giving a young man lessons in Greek each Saturday. It has taken about all day, and with all my college work has kept me very busy. I have had two junior speeches already, and there are still more. Several girls from Flint tried to have me go home with them for the vacation, but I made up my mind to stay and do what I could for myself and the other people here. A young Mr. M. is going to recite to me every day in Virgil; so with teaching and all the rest I shan't have time to be homesick, though it will seem rather lonely when the other girls are gone and I don't hear the college bell for two weeks.

My mission school is prosperous, though I found my class pretty badly demoralized by the vacation. It has been hard work pulling it into order again. Two missionaries from Turkey are here, one a graduate of this university. He spoke in the hall last night to an audience of two thousand. I met him yesterday and had a good deal of talk with him, and he was in all my recitations to-day. He says, " We want you, Miss Freeman, in Central Turkey; " Professor D'Ooge adds, " We want you in the United States." They have finally concluded to leave it to me; and I don't believe I'm wanted very badly anywhere.

This week has been one of the saddest I have spent here, notwithstanding the fact that Miss S. is getting well. She is now so much better that there is little doubt of her entire recovery, and she will soon go home. I sat up all night with her Wednesday. The girls take turns in looking after her, which we shan't need to do much longer. But death has come among us this week. Mr. C. of '75 was one of my good friends. Last year he was elected President of our Lecture Association, the highest office of the senior class. Dr. Angell says he was the foremost man in his class. I came to know him in the Association, where he was very prominent. He was preparing for the ministry. A week ago he was at the prayer meeting and afterwards talked to me earnestly of his plans for next winter. He lives only a few miles from here and goes home every Saturday. As he started for home last week he remarked to a friend that he was not feeling quite well; and almost before we had missed him news came on Tuesday that he was dead. Brain fever did its work in three days, and carried off one of the noblest men I shall ever know. His class went in a body to the funeral and the entire university is completely shocked.

Ottawa

My first week here was hard. Of course there are many things to get used to, and so many strange names and faces to put together. But it will all grow easier after a time, and I have been feeling pretty well. I begin at nine in the morning and end at half-past four. Then I have my registers and class books to arrange, and so don't go home until supper time. After that I have eight lessons to prepare for the next day, which, when I'm tired, costs some effort. I try to spend the entire evening on these; only I have had calls every evening so far, which takes time, you know. Friday nights I arrange the standing of each one and count the absences. If these amount to three half days, I send a note to the parents. Once a week we have essays, declamations, and select readings; and Saturday afternoons I have essays to criticise. Then I board three quarters of a mile from the school, and that takes time, but I like it. Saturday I got at my merino dress, put a new braid on, and sewed all the evening as hard as possible. I don't know when I have improved every minute as I have been obliged to here. It is a very good thing. I had such an abominable habit of wasting time, and I'm likely to get cured. You must tell me all about our classes and what is doing each week. I get so hungry to hear it all. I just devoured your letter. Do tell me the little things.

Yesterday an Irishman living in this street, while drunk, struck his wife with an ax, hitting her over the head, in fact pounded her almost to death. She was in terrible pain. A neighbor called the doctor, who was with her till she died just before noon; but he could do little for her. There's no doubt that her husband killed her. What is worse, she herself drank almost as much as he, and was a very bad woman. There's one little boy. Oh, L.! Don't you wish we could stop this dreadful liquor selling? That's where the blame lies. If I were a man, would n't I do something? Come to think of it, I should n't wonder if I should as it is.

Your letter came Wednesday in a terrible snowstorm, itself almost like a great snowflake, and made me want to go to you. For a while I felt as if I must put my arms about you and try to comfort you. But I could only come up here by myself and pray that the dear Christ, who loves and pities you, would give you peace and rest. After all, I am afraid that is all I can ever do. Perhaps it is the most any of us can do for each other, no matter what our love may be. But you are not " all alone." Don't ever say so. " Lo, I am with you always, even unto the end." I think of you so often this hard examination week, so much harder now when you are sick — body and soul. Do be just as happy as you can, in any way you can. You have found that fighting yourself does no good, that in the unequal contest you are trying to crush what each day shows you is a part of your very soul. No! Shun everything that hurts you. Be good to yourself always and everywhere. You have n't any too much strength. But if you carry your cross, you may obtain strength from it for the onward journey. So take it in and let it help and soothe you, even though you know it to be a dream.

Such a dreadful thing has happened! A letter of two sheets came from Mr. W. this week; and oh, such a letter! It just takes my breath away, it hurts me so to think of it. Why, why is it that I seem doomed to the very thing I would most be delivered from? I never imagined it in him, did you? I must answer it to-day, and it does n't seem as if I could. It is such a passionate letter, and I know he must be terribly in earnest to talk so. I tremble for the effect it will have on him just now. Do be kind to him, if you have any chance. And here is Mr. S. walking home from class with me every evening. I moved, you know, to get away for a little while from worry of this sort. And of course I don't mean to say such an absurd thing as that he is really in danger. Only he is too kind. But I am getting suspicious of everybody who looks at me, unless I have been introduced to his wife.

I finished yesterday just half the weeks I have to teach, and the ten that are left will pass too quickly, doubtless, for the work which is to be done in them; but not when I think where the end of them will take me. Once in a while I dread going back to college. Not that it is n't far pleasanter than teaching. But sometimes the world seems sick. I can't help thinking of what you told me of the secret societies. God help us all! He alone is able. Let us pray for the noble young men who are going down unless an arm mighty to save is quickly thrown around them. So S. has gone too! I liked the boy so much. Perhaps it is better for him. But what a loss to the class! Really in a year there won't be much of a class left, at this rate. Oh, if we could only sit down and talk it all over!

Mother, this being off alone, so out in the world, is tiresome; the more so because my life is crowded with work and care. But I am succeeding. There was a meeting of the Board this week, and the President afterwards informed me that "they were all grateful to me for what I was doing for the school.

And though from the first I had given them to understand that I was here only for the year, they begged me to reconsider the matter;" in short, telling me I must stay. I told him as politely as I knew how that I could n't and should n't, and they still insist. They say I know enough now and can finish my studies by myself. As if they knew! Well! I hope they won't be disappointed before the year is out.

V

SCHOOL-TEACHING

When a young person leaves college, where for four years he has been supported while happily pursuing his own ends, and goes forth into an alien world which demands as its price for his living that he shall attend to its needs, the change is disturbing. In college the aims of culture and enjoyment are dominant; in the world outside there is the necessity of watching others' wants; our own preferences drop a good deal out of sight. Accordingly it is often said that a college unfits one for practical life. Though it gives the means of becoming broadly serviceable, it does not necessarily bring the desire, and certainly does not form the requisite habits. What we gain in college is apt enough to stick fast within us, and not easily to pass beyond. Before we can succeed in the new and dutiful ways our aims need readjusting. For most persons there comes something of a jolt in turning from the period of acquisition to that of distribution. In Miss Freeman's case this was less violent on account of her early training and the austere conditions which attended her college life. Yet even she found the years immediately after leaving college severe. From 1876 to 1881 she went through much exhausting drudgery: she was overworked and underpaid, she was imperfectly fed, she had too little fresh air and amusement, she was burdened with family anxieties, and was sent hither and thither with little power to choose the place where she would be. The beginnings of professional life make little account of personal desires. The years 1876-87, therefore, from graduation to her marriage, I group together as a third period of her career and call it her time of service. In her second period, from her entering Windsor Academy to her leaving the University of Michigan, she was — though with many distractions — accumulating knowledge and properly serving her own ends. Now, what others require becomes her chief care, and she is mainly busied with expenditure.

At Lake Geneva, Wisconsin, was a seminary for girls, whose ages ranged from twelve to twenty-five. Its head was a college acquaintance of Miss Freeman's, and two of her classmates were engaged as teachers. She herself agreed to take charge of the Greek and Latin on a nominal salary of eight hundred dollars. Part of this was conditional on the success of the school; three hundred dollars was charged to the tuition of her sister Ella, who, having just become engaged, now needed good general training rather than a college course. The actual profits of the undertaking were therefore small. The summer had to be spent in preparing her sister and herself for the new work. In the midst of it the youngest sister, Stella, fell seriously ill, while the financial prospects of the family grew steadily darker. There was a gloom upon her when she went to Lake Geneva which increased the hardships of the early weeks there. She writes: —

"A month ago I took the severest cold I have had for years. It went to my lungs, and for some days made me decidedly sick. I am better now. But one does n't get entire rest in teaching at a boarding school, even when one is well. I am far from that. You know I did n't rest during the summer, and I have n't rested for a good while. When I came here, weary and sad, I threw myself into my work; for I found many perplexities and difficulties. So long as my time was taken in working against these, I did not feel the weakness which crept over me after I began to see more 'open doors' about and ahead of me. The work itself is n't so very hard. I ought to grow strong in it. But I am not used to boarding school life. Being 'slave to a bell and vassal to an hour' is irksome sometimes when my heart longs for other scenes and the friends from whose presence I have gone away. My roommate is a refined, talented, and pleasant person of thirty; and yet I would so much rather be alone. You ask if I am happy. Let me be honest with you to-night. No, I am not. But I am content, and that is better. I am at work, and before me stretch high aims and great tasks, more than enough to fill the years until I shall awake in His likeness and be satisfied."

But these were not Miss Freeman's usual moods. The sense of human needs in the school soon engaged her, and a fair degree of health returned. Of the way in which her ideals of teaching were taking shape a good notion may be had from a letter written at this time to one of her friends, who was herself a teacher:

"You ask how I work among the girls to gain influence. Let me talk to you a little about it. As I lived among these young people day after day, I felt a want of something: not intellectual, or even religious, culture; not a lack of physical training or that acquaintance with social life which can be so charming in a true woman; but a something I must call heart culture, in lack of a better name. Every one was kind, but cold. There was no intentional freezing, but an absence of the sunshine which melts its own way. Looking on and into them, I said, I will try to be a friend to them *all*, and put all that is truest and sweetest, sunniest and strongest that I can gather into their lives. While I teach them solid knowledge, and give them real school drill as faithfully as I may, I will give, too, all that the years have brought to my own soul. God help me to give what

He gave — myself — and make that self worth something to somebody; teach me to love all as He has loved, for the sake of the infinite possibilities locked up in every human soul. Consecrating myself to the future of these girls, to them as women, I have tried in this life among them to make them feel that they can always come to me in happy and in sad times, in restless moments, or homesick and tired hours. Whenever they want help or comfort, my door and heart shall be open. Not that I have said this. I have just felt it, and I think they feel it too. We kneel together every evening, and every morning at chapel service their faces look up into mine. Keeping my eyes open for chances, I find the rest takes care of itself — a word, a look even, the touch of a hand; and by and by, when the time comes, something more. I have to work very differently here from what was possible in Ann Arbor. A university town has food which you can't give boarding-school girls, nor men and women of still less culture; and these make up the majority of a town like this, though we have some families as cultivated and wealthy as can be found anywhere. But Christianity meets the wants of every heart; only it takes experience, knowledge of and insight into human nature — but far more than anything else, the spirit of Christ himself — in order to know when and how to speak. Why, what is it to be a Christian, a Christ-follower, unless it is going about doing good? We ought to love everybody and make everybody love us. Then everything else is easy."

Such a teacher does not fail. Miss Freeman was pressed to continue another year. But the atmosphere of a private school was never quite congenial to her. Its little proprieties, its small interests, its narrow intellectual horizon, were matters distasteful to her free soul, and yet she was powerless to change them. If she were to teach the following year, she preferred to do so in a public school, where there would be both boys and girls. But dreams of wider scope were running in her head. Throughout her college course she had hoped for a period of graduate study; and she felt this especially important in view of the interruption of her junior year. She longed to repair that loss, as well as the damage done by the crowded freshman time. In the early seventies, too, the degree of Doctor of Philosophy was just beginning to assert its haughty claims, and was felt doubly desirable by those who had little opportunity for undergraduate electives. History was her favorite study. It dealt with persons. Her imagination illuminated it and she followed with enthusiasm its vast moral evolutions. Then, too, always and everywhere she loved a fact. Foreseeing that most of her solid years must be given to teaching, she seems to have formed some project of devoting summer vacations, and later perhaps a single entire year, to advanced study. Immediately on leaving Lake Geneva she accordingly began work on an historical subject at Ann Arbor. I find the following memorandum in her hand: "June–Sept., 1877. Spent the summer in Ann Arbor studying for a higher degree. Did not return for examinations the following year on account of Stella's illness. Was offered an instructorship in mathematics at Wellesley College, but declined." The plan of advanced study was never abandoned. From time to time, as other toils permitted, it was resumed; and though her thesis was never completed, in 1882 the university conferred on her the degree of Ph.D.

As the official head of education in that state, the University of Michigan interests itself in the welfare of all its high schools. One of these at Saginaw, in Northern Michigan, had fallen into decay. Its principal, a man of loveable character, was incapable of keeping order. The scholarship of the school had therefore for some time been declining until, though it still had several hundred pupils, it was of diminishing value to the university and the town. The superintendent of schools consulted President Angell. He advised that the kindly principal be nominally retained, but that Miss Freeman be appointed preceptress and left to smooth out the difficulties of the situation in whatever way her tact could devise. Thither she accordingly went in September, 1877;

and a month later, on the resignation of another teacher, she secured a position for her sister Ella as the head of a neighboring grammar school. The contest for authority in her own school was at first sharp. The leader of the organized turbulence was a young man of about her own years; for she was only twenty-two, slight, and in feeble health. Within a week she had turned him out of school and did not readmit him until he had made public apology. Within two months all friction had disappeared, the standard of scholarship was raised, teachers and pupils were alike friendly. She had won regard from the people of Saginaw, and at the end of the year a hundred dollars of additional salary was gratuitously voted her. I have talked with pupils of that school, who cannot comprehend how anything less than magic could in a few weeks have changed so rude a company as themselves into sweet-natured and diligent students.

But this time of sunny peacemaking was a season of anguish for herself. The health of her sister in New York still failed. Stella, the youngest of the family, was regarded by all as its choicest member. Her starry beauty was remarked everywhere. She wrote delightfully in prose and verse, was a capital story-teller, witty, studious, high-minded, less stormy in temper than Alice, and up to her fifteenth year apparently in vigorous health. Then the family weakness showed itself. An attack of fever settled in her lungs and could not be dislodged. Alice nursed her through the first summer vacation after she left college, and expected the trouble to disappear. It did not, however; consumption declared itself, and for two years fears and hopes chased one another perplexingly. In the autumn of 1877 doctors pronounced the illness dangerous, and began to talk of a change of climate. All these distresses, too, were complicated with financial troubles. The lumber entanglement, which I have mentioned before as dragging the family down, had gone from bad to worse, until Dr. Freeman believed he could best protect his creditors by giving up to them his home and all his property. This occurred in November, 1877, just as Alice and Ella had begun their teaching in Saginaw.

The two girls speedily set about plans of relief. Their joint salaries amounted to eleven hundred dollars, and there were hopes of increasing this a little by private pupils. They hired and furnished a house, and at Christmas had the entire family settled in Saginaw. The expenses of a loved invalid are always heavy, and it was not easy to meet them in the midst of school problems. But the father soon began practice as a physician, the mother took a teacher or two to board, and the son found a place in a store. All had brave hearts. Throughout the winter the family was happy in one another and in a common care.

By summer Stella was so much revived that Ella was able to marry, and the brother to enter the Medical School of the University of Michigan. But as the second winter approached, the fair prospects darkened; and Alice, who had been called to Wellesley again in December, 1878, — this time in Greek, — felt that she must once more decline. The beautiful sufferer lingered till Spring, but died on June 20, 1879, at the age of eighteen. No other grief of Mrs. Palmer's life equalled this. Stella was five years younger than she and had been much in her charge. She loved her as her own child and also as one whom she thought superior to herself. She dreamed of one day sending her to college, and of their becoming ultimately associated in some common work. No death had hitherto come near her, and this one made all which subsequently came seem slight. As she herself lay dying, I heard her murmur Stella's name.

It was well to leave Saginaw now. A change of surroundings was equally necessary for health and for work. Dr. Freeman's practice, too, was increasing, and the family was once more on its feet. Her brother had been sent to college; her surviving sister was married and gone to her own home. On herself a third call to Wellesley was pressed, a call of a higher kind than before. She had been in correspondence about it for several months, putting the proposal aside at first because she would not leave her sister. By that sister's death she was sorrowfully set free. In July, 1879, when she was twenty-four, she became the head of the department of history at Wellesley College.

I suppose I must give a few poignant glimpses into the two years' life in Saginaw, years which began in gladness and ran into continually deeper tragedy. Without them Miss Freeman cannot be known. She was a hardened optimist, and because of her cheerful courage she appeared to many like a favorite of fortune on whom good things regularly fell. Fortunate indeed she was, but chiefly in her power of discovering a soul of good in things evil. Hope in her view is —

> The paramount duty that Heaven lays
> For its own honor on man's suffering heart.

Yet I must let it be seen that she had her full share of hardships and was abundantly acquainted with grief. Moods of despondency came to her as truly as to others, and she did not hesitate to express them. I have purposely included several such utterances among her letters. But she was not absorbed or misled by them. She went straight on. General Grant remarks, in his "Memoirs," that all soldiers are frightened about equally on going into battle, but that there is a mighty difference in the way they behave under fear. She had a sensitive heart, and to feel her humanity we must see it quiver. But she put her mind elsewhere than in her moods, and these soon took their suitable place. To duty she gave herself gladly, counting it the voice of a friend, and in its exhilarating companionship she found a way through even physical ills. Her "radiance" was therefore no product of ignorance, but of a deeper insight into things human and divine. She often quoted some lines of Emerson's which well describe her own mode of meeting good and ill; only she understood them as expressing no mere Stoicism but the Christian's joyous acceptance of a complex and hallowed world: —

> Let me go where'er I will,
> I hear a sky-born music still.
> It sounds from all things old,
> It sounds from all things young;
> From all that 's fair, from all that 's foul,
> Peals out a cheerful song.
> It is not only in the rose,
> It is not only in the bird,
> Not only where the rainbow glows,
> Nor in the song of woman heard;
> But in the darkest, meanest things,
> There alway, alway, something sings.

LETTERS

Across the table sits my queenly sister, reading a letter with flushing cheeks. She came a week ago to take a position which the superintendent obtained for her in a grammar school. Is n't everybody kind to me? And we have had such talks about those at home whom I have n't seen in so long. Our room is bright and cozy, and we hope to have a happy year. Just now my hands are so full of monthly examinations and reports that my usual labors in mathematics and the sciences seem too trivial to mention.

How sunny and restful your letter sounds to-day, when I am so tired. Friday night my school closes for two weeks. That evening my father, mother, and Stella arrive. The week after, the State Teachers' Association meets here for three days. During those days and in the mean time I shall be driven with work, as I have five classes which will be examined for the benefit of these visitors. Then in the vacation I must get my family settled. I have already rented a house, but probably it will be no light matter to put it in order for the winter.

To you I don't mind explaining what would otherwise seem a little mysterious in our arrangements. Two months ago Papa made an assignment of everything to his creditors. When this business was over, it seemed best that there should be an immediate change. One of Papa's lungs has failed, and Stella is no better. So I am to have them here with me. Fred will come soon. I am very anxious that he should enter the Medical School next fall. And

Ella must have next year for study and rest, as she will undoubtedly be married the year after.

Forgive me, then, for having written so little. I have been in constant communication with the assignee and have had much to do for Ella. My duties, too, at the school are so numerous that I go every morning at eight o'clock and for the last two weeks have remained until dark. It has been damp, and I have not felt very well. But won't it be pleasant for us to be together again at Christmas? The first time I have seen the family in the winter since 1871. Please say nothing about these perplexities of mine. I don't want anybody to think a troubled thought of me. I really don't need such thoughts. I can see a little way ahead now, and am quite willing to trust and work.

The spring-time is without and within. It has come early this year, and how beautiful! Yesterday Ella and Stella and I went out walking as the sun was rising. The air seems like April's, and the sunshine like June's, while here and there a bird sings cheerily from branches just swelling and reddening. We walked about three miles, and came home perfectly ravenous.

You see by this how much better Stella is. Since coming here she has greatly improved, indeed is better now than she has been since last summer.

Next term she is going to study, if she continues so strong. She plans to go to the school each morning for practice in writing. I am still doubtful about it. But she is so restless, she must try at any rate. This morning we all went to church together, for the first time in so long that it seems like going away back or away onward, I hardly know which.

It is only a fortnight since our wedding and you are looking forward to your own. Naturally I have been thinking a good deal about the two. I wish we could have the whole afternoon for a talk. But do keep happy, and grow wise in keeping another happy. Be unselfish, dear, and learn to control the woman's restless hunger. Let it only make you more sympathetic and strong. Sympathy is the great want of the human heart, man's heart as well as woman's. You must teach him how to sympathize in the broad sense with you, and to let you sympathize with him, in little as well as great things. Then you will feel always that you are bound up together, that everything you each do is full of the other. That, I think, must be being married; and that, you know, is n't the work of an hour, or a year. Then, no matter what comes, you can never be really separated. Shakespeare understood this when he wrote his sonnets.

All this week my thoughts have been following

you, this busy week of organizing our high school. I want you here, these white still nights. Last night I sat till late, looking out into the beauty of the moonlight and thinking of friends. I was going over the years that are past and wondered why so many things, buried long ago with the dead years, rise up and sit down beside me in the silence. There are days when every air blows from a distance. This house is haunted nowadays. Sometimes I long for one of those moments that are gone more than for all that the days to come hold in their close-shut hands.

I am hungry to hear from you. I seem so shut-in this year. Home and school life keep me so occupied that I have hardly been able to give a moment to anything outside, except when too tired to do anything but think. These times have come oftener than they used to. Just now I am oppressed with the passing days. Do you know, lately I have come to want to paint flowers and all sorts of lovely things, to sketch faces that are pleasant to me. You have genius for this. I should have to learn. Had I better try? I do so want to be putting bright bits of beauty into and out of my life. Stella is having a high fever this afternoon. I must go to her.

Sometimes in these days it seems as if the solid earth were giving way under my feet, as if all my present and future were slipping out of my control. And then I turn instinctively to my past. I suppose that is what God gives us a past for, to stand on. We are sure now that we can keep Stella only a little while. The fight has been so long we hardly know how to give it up. But we cannot expect her to endure through the summer. She grows whiter and weaker every day, suffering intensely. Our light is dying out. Pray the good God to lighten and warm this dark home, where we watch her going farther away from our helpless help.

These days are solemnly sweet. I make no plans in them. Recently I have written Mr. Durant about the state of things here, but have not had his reply. You see it is extremely doubtful whether I go to Wellesley. Nothing is clear before me now. I am very tired. The year has worn upon me, in school and at home. But I think I shall come through without breaking down. If I do go to Wellesley, I have promised Mr. Durant to go at the earliest moment. He wants me to do some studying there, and has been urging me to resign here. The position certainly requires much preparation, and I must consult about methods and books.

School ended last week; and though my work is not quite finished, vacation is begun. I am not altogether well — nothing serious, only too tired to sleep, and sometimes too heartsick to want to rest. I am going to leave Saginaw just as soon as I can get ready, next week I think. Before going to Wellesley I shall spend a few days in Windsor. I have n't been there in three years, and must stay a little with those who knew us when we were children. It will do me good to rest in the old places among the hills. But I go soon to Wellesley, because I must see what books are in the library there. I have to arrange my topics and make my references, as the classes use no text-books. Forgive me for not writing you more. The silence of death has fallen upon my life. It is a very quiet time within, but O Lucy, Lucy! — Well dear, good-by. Send me a letter out of your beautiful life as soon as you can. Kiss me, Lucy, and hold me close to keep my heart from breaking.

VI

TEACHING AT WELLESLEY

WELLESLEY COLLEGE, to which Miss Freeman went in 1879, and with which she was connected for the next eight years, was opened in 1875 by Henry Fowle Durant. He had graduated at Harvard College in 1841, entered the law in Boston, and soon won eminence and a fortune by his masterly conduct of difficult cases in the courts. Slight in stature and imperious in will, he took pleasure in contest and easily made strong friends and strong enemies. There was about him great personal charm. He had read much, had an excellent library, wrote with refinement in prose and verse, and was something of a connoisseur in the arts. Near the close of his brilliant and contentious life he lost a son of remarkable promise. The shock turned his attention to religious matters. Into these he threw himself with his customary ardor, retiring from the law. To rid himself of self-seeking and to make his property and his remaining years a benefit to his fellow men became his passion. These purposes were warmly seconded by his wife. It was their belief that a community could be helped most by education, and they deter-

WELLESLEY COLLEGE
as seen from Lake Waban

mined to express their affection for their son by founding a college. On examining the provision for education already made in our Eastern States, they concluded that women were in greater need than men. Vassar had just been opened and was the only considerable college for girls, though of colleges from which women were excluded New England had more than a dozen. By enlarging the opportunities for women Mr. and Mrs. Durant thought they could best accomplish their generous purpose. Their home was at Wellesley, fifteen miles west of Boston, where they had an estate of more than three hundred acres, made up of plains, hills, woods, and the shores of Lake Waban. This they now deeded to trustees as the site of the new college,—Mr. Durant directing, however, that neither it nor any of its buildings should be called by his name, nor should any portrait of himself be hung within its walls.

It will be seen that there was religious ardor in the founding of Wellesley, and a spirit of sacrifice, qualities without which few endowments undertaken for the public good prove permanently strong. At the beginning the fervor of a young convert may have led Mr. Durant to give undue prominence to the conscious religious motive; but he kept all doors open for the extensive changes which time has proved wise, and in his holiest injunctions there was great sagacity. The college was to be Christian, but no sect was to have a majority of its trustees. All its officials were to be devout persons, but not bound by any form of subscription. With clear understanding of the native tendencies of womanhood, the motto, "Not to be ministered unto but to minister" was selected for the college seal. Morning and evening there were twenty-minute periods of "Silent Time," when each girl must be alone in her room, and devotions would be natural, though not enforced. Required prayers twice a day were led by the teachers, Sunday services by invited ministers, and there were daily Bible classes. From among the professors advisers were appointed for each class, who kept regular office hours and were accessible for consultation on any subject. It must be remembered that in those days parents were little inclined to separate their daughters from family influence, and that many features of the home had to be provided if girls were to be drawn to the higher education.

It is to Mr. Durant's credit that at a time when such things were less regarded than at present he laid great stress on the beauty of surroundings, spending much on his grounds, on paintings and photographs, on music, on whatever might ennoble the young through unconscious influence. And while he very properly sought to develop Christian character in his college, it was not his purpose to substitute this for intellectual discipline. Determined that the standard of scholarship should ultimately be the highest, he attached little weight to text-books, made generous provision for laboratories and library, and favored methods of teaching which were quite in advance of his time. Of course such purposes could not be realized at once. In every beginning there is chaos. He was himself but slenderly acquainted with educational matters, and there were few highly trained women to form his faculty. Women he preferred as professors, because hitherto they had not been allowed to teach in colleges; and girls were little likely to become students if told that there was something in their sex which debarred them from high scientific standing.

It was to a college thus nobly conceived that Alice Freeman came, a college for which all her previous training had prepared her and which was planned to embody most of her own ideals. Yet perhaps it is not unfair to say that, while Mr. Durant was its founder, she in her brief term was its builder. The ideas were his; but they were hers too, and they waited for her to disclose the modes of so applying them as to give them power over the future. Had the aim of the college been simply scholastic, she might have been stifled. Had it been careless of scholarship, she would not have remained. But seeking as it did to fashion beautiful women, she identified herself with it enthusiastically, in herself embodied its type, and by degrees constructed a Wellesley spirit in which helpfulness, modesty, intelligence, and grace are recognized ingredients.

The attention of Mr. Durant was first drawn to her by President Angell. Of the circumstances he gives the following account, not knowing apparently how long the negotiations were in progress, and probably fixing the date a year later than it really was:—

"When Mr. Durant founded Wellesley College so few women had received college education that he experienced some difficulty in finding suitable candidates for the professorial chairs. On my recommendation he appointed three or four Michigan graduates, who proved so satisfactory that he wrote to me to inform him at any time when we graduated such a woman as I thought he ought to appoint. It so happened that I had occasion, I think in the year 1879, to visit the high school in East Saginaw, of which Miss Freeman was then principal. I attended a class in English Literature which she was teaching. The class was composed of boys of from fifteen to eighteen years of age, in whom one would perhaps hardly expect much enthusiasm for the great masters of English literature. But it was soon apparent that she had those boys, as she always had her classes, completely under her control and largely filled with her own enthusiasm. They showed that at their homes they had been carefully and lovingly reading some of the great masterpieces and were ready to discuss them with intelligence and zest. I have never witnessed finer work of the kind with a class of that sort. When I returned home, I wrote to Mr. Durant that he *must* appoint the woman whose remarkable work I had been witnessing, that he could not afford to let her slip out of his hand. Whether my letter led to his decision to call her to Wellesley I do not know. But he did call her, and she went. The rest is matter of history."

Of her success as a teacher it is hardly necessary to speak. The interest which she aroused in history is well known. She gave it a freshness and vitality which have become traditional at Wellesley, and so organized her department that it has remained one of the most influential in the college. But where the time was found for study and planning I cannot discover. She must have lived at a killing pace. From her note-books I find that her regular work consisted of fifteen hours a week of history, a daily Bible class, charge of a portion of the domestic work, office hours each day as adviser to the senior class, and the oversight of her assistant in history. To this she added once a week throughout the winter a public lecture on some historical subject. All this work, too, was carried on in the grief and bodily weakness caused by her sister's death. In the same note-books I find the following fragmentary entries: —

"Jan. 8. Faculty meeting after Chapel. A lovely day. I walked to the village and was out of doors an hour. Wrote letters and corrected examination papers. Spent an hour or more over new books on the Bible. It's so hard to do neglected work! — Jan. 10. Enthusiastic sections this morning, and history classes this afternoon unusually good. Fanny W. went to French table and Mary P. took her place at mine. I am going to have the girls change their seats once a week. Read German with my reading circle. — Jan. 13. Everything has gone wrong to-day. My Roman history did not do well this morning. Worked in the Library on references. Could not get exercise, but had a little sleep this afternoon. Must improve at once in health and work. — Jan. 19. A beautiful day, but full of disappointments and downright badness. When shall I conquer my besetting sins? Wasted the evening with Emily, Marion, Helen, and Jane."

Evidently too much work had been assigned her, an error perhaps inevitable in the early years of a college. Mr. Durant's fortune was limited, while the demands upon it were not. Out of his own pocket he met whatever bills were in excess of the income from tuition, and this was fixed at a low figure. For many years, until other donors could be found, there was hard work and small pay. Then too the practice of attending not only to the studies of students, but also to their character and manners is, as the English universities have learned, a time-taking business. An enormous amount of Miss Freeman's time was spent in interviews with girls, interviews often of lifelong benefit to the girl herself and certainly the most efficient means of creating an understanding of what the college should be; but more than anything else these ate up her time and strength. We now know that not much administrative work can safely be put on a teacher. But this was not so well understood at that time, and it is not strange that one who had aptitudes in both directions should have been overstrained.

In its initial steps an undertaking usually requires a single strong hand. Mr. Durant was naturally autocratic, and during the few years of his life he ruled Wellesley absolutely, within and without. He had, it is true, appointed Miss Ada L. Howard president; but her duties as an executive officer were rather nominal than real; neither his disposition, her health, nor her previous training allowing her much power. Even the Board of Trustees exercised little real control. Mr. Durant held all the authority, and his keen eye early discovered the force of Miss Freeman. In her first year he said to one of the trustees, "You see that little dark-eyed girl? She will be the next president of Wellesley." Though frequently they did not agree, her independence did not alienate him, but appeared to make him trust her the more. He loved the strong. Often he sought her out, talked with her on historical and literary matters, explored her ideas of teaching, and bore from her opposition which others feared to give. The prophecy of her future rise which I have just quoted was made shortly after the following clash.

Mr. Durant had called her attention to a member of the senior class as one "who was not a Christian," and directed Miss Freeman to go and talk with her "about her soul." He was a man already past fifty, accustomed to be obeyed, and she a girl of twenty-four; but she flatly refused. He demanded her reasons. She explained how disrespectful such direct assaults on one's personality are, and how generally ineffective. She said that to do such a thing would be contrary to her whole mode of intercourse with students and might well shake their confidence in her. In short, she would not do it. He insisted, and for a time she feared the resistance would cost her her place. But after the painful affair was over he never referred to it again, except by treating her with ever-increasing trust. On her side, too, admiration for Mr. Durant held firm through all their differences, and ceased only with her life.

Yet this incident will indicate some of the perplexities which filled the early years when, under its masterful leader, the hastily gathered college was learning to organize itself. Such things cost blood. So did the immense load of her teaching. So did the penetrating personal influence of which she was so lavish. So did her longing for her dead sister. So did the efforts she was making to help her brother through college. Such a person confines herself to no single care, nor accepts ease when exhaustion requires it; but, hiding her inner bleedings from herself as well as from others, carries for their sake a group of interwoven anxieties.

Such at least was Miss Freeman's prodigality at this time. Later she learned, though she always found it difficult, a larger generosity. Never sturdy, she came to Wellesley in broken health and had no time to repair it. The cough which she took from Windsor to Ann Arbor grew constantly more racking, until in February, 1880, a hemorrhage of the lungs occurred. It was the busiest time of the year, and she at first persuaded Dr. Bowditch to let her continue work until the spring recess. But on fuller examination he ordered her off at once, advising Southern France, and saying that probably she had but six months to live. She turned to Windsor, and on the way through New York consulted Dr. Willard Parker. I find a note in which she has recorded, "Dr. Parker tells me I can live if I have character and courage enough." He made her feel the recklessness of ways of living which she had previously thought necessary; he sent her to the open air, to exercises in breathing, to hygiene, food, and care. She went to the old farm and took herself resolutely in hand. By isolation, energy, and healthful surroundings, she refitted herself so that she was able to return to Wellesley in April, after the spring recess, and to carry her full work until the end of the term. The summer brought further invigoration. Thus at the very outset of her career she was seemingly crippled; but accepting the disaster in her usual optimistic way, she drew from it such knowledge of the laws of health as turned her into a vigorous woman. When she was examined eight years later the lesion had entirely disappeared, nor did it ever return.

But the unorganized conditions at Wellesley proved dangerous to others beside herself. Mr. Durant was slowly sinking throughout 1880 and 1881, and in October of the latter year he died. About the same time Miss Howard's feeble health altogether gave way and compelled her to resign. A meeting of the Trustees was held on November 15, and Miss Freeman was appointed vice-president, but acting president for the year. Though she was the youngest professor then in service, and so far as I can learn the youngest that has ever been appointed there, she had already so proved her power that the judgment of the Faculty went with that of the Trustees. Being unwilling to withdraw altogether from her courses in history, she continued a portion of her teaching for a time, but also entered immediately on her executive work.

When the surprising election was communicated to Miss Freeman, only a few hours could be allowed her for deliberation. The following account of how she spent those hours is furnished by a former Wellesley teacher and confirmed from an independent source: "When the question of accepting the presidency was presented to her for immediate decision, she took her horse and drove away quite alone over quiet country roads, so deep in thought that she noticed nothing about her until she found herself miles away, somewhere beyond South Framingham. When most young women would have consumed the time in asking advice of older persons whose experience would have been of little service, she, like St. Paul, conferred not with flesh and blood, but sought the solitary place and communed with her own soul."

I have already shown the necessarily disturbed condition of the college in these early years. There were now fears of trouble from the more than usually animated senior class. They had intimations of the election almost as soon as Miss Freeman learned it herself, and were much elated over the prospect of being ruled by a president but little older than themselves. When Miss Freeman returned to her rooms, she sent for this class. They came in a body, filling with their merry presence all her chairs, tables, and floor. She told them she had called them together because she needed their advice. She had been asked that day to become acting president of Wellesley. She was too young for the office. Indeed, its duties were too heavy for any one. If she must meet them alone, she would have to decline. But it had occurred to her that perhaps they would be willing to take part with her, looking after the order of the college themselves, and leaving her free for general administration. If they were ready to undertake this, she thought she might accept. Of course the response was hearty. They voted themselves her assistants on the spot, and difficult indeed it was for any member of the three lower classes to stray from the straight path that year. I once asked Mrs. Palmer how she managed to survive the severities of a first presidential year, and she answered that she could not have done it if she had not had the help of the seniors. Of the instantaneous resourcefulness which secured her that help she said nothing. This I have learned since her death from a member of the class.

LETTERS

Clara D. has just been in my room, all excited over Jacob and Esau. "Jacob was such a selfish wretch to steal that birthright." She delights in getting herself wrought up, and I decidedly disapprove it. She tires her friends, and I am careful not to let her draw upon my strength unduly. In fact it is my principle here not to be intimate with any of the girls or to let them waste much of my time. Unless you are careful in this great family, all your time goes uselessly. You accomplish nothing. I think Mr. Durant expects his teachers to give themselves boundlessly to the girls; but I can't do that this year even if I don't "make them adore me," as he says I must. It is a good thing for my health to be unpopular enough to be let alone, and I shan't try to be anything else. What do you think of that?

I don't know what to do about a watch. Our recitations are partly lectures, partly notes, and partly questions. So I must have some guide in time, and none is provided here. Fifty dollars will get me as good a one as I shall ever need. But I am not paid until October. Perhaps I can get along until then. Only there are F.'s college expenses. Mother, could you meet those bills at present and let me send the money later?

Nobody is so much what she ought to be as a good girl, if only people would let her alone. One of the freshmen has just left me after an hour of eager talk. She has a wonderfully bright, attractive mind, sensitive but timid, afraid lest her "sins are too stultifying to leave enough soul to be worth saving." How I like to talk of these things with such girls, so honest and simple, so unwilling to run any risk of shirking duty or failing of the truth! If we could only trust God and lead natural, simple lives! This child's mind is full of what men — Presbyterians of Albany — have been telling her about God's ways, and therefore of much that is both unreasonable and hopeless. But we have had a good hour, and she sees that a religious life does n't consist in feeling either great sorrow for sin or great exaltation and rapture over forgiveness. How patient God is with us all! I wonder at it more and more, when he has so much to tell, and we such slowness in understanding.

I have just sent the girls out of my room, telling them they must give me a chance to write a birthday letter to my father. The truth is, an individual girl is a lovely and bewitching creature, but five hundred come to be a trifle — just a trifle — tiresome once in a long time. As old age comes on, I am afraid I shall grow homesick. Certainly I have never wished so much to be at home as this last year. Don't you think it would be nice to settle down somewhere and enjoy life awhile? When shall we begin? When Christmas comes I am going home. I really can't stay away longer. But remember I am very well this year, and all things here seem harmonious and prosperous. God keep them so!

It is "Silent Time," and all the house is still. I will write to you instead of reading my Bible. I have just come from one of the little talks I am giving on Fridays. For two evenings my recitation room has been so crowded that the girls have stood in the corridor as far as they could hear. Now they have asked me to go up to the large lecture room. This talk about my "lectures" makes me feel cheap. But to-night I promised to go there for the next time. I was speaking on Dante, and several of the teachers came. Next week the subject is Savonarola. We are arousing some interest in history. There's need enough. You can't think how discouraged I sometimes am.

I am spending these holidays at home and find them like a pleasant dream, full of little house-talks, of neighbors dropping in, of rides and drives and long walks, and here and there a touch of business. One morning was taken up by a gentleman who insisted on my writing an English history! He will give me two years to do it. The publishers will make any terms I may name. A bright little woman has a book that she wishes me "to edit in order to insure its sale." What a queer world it is! And the same day good Mrs. O. comes to get me to drive six miles to her Industrial School. But a college friend is also here for the day, and he gives her five dollars for her school in order to have my company for the afternoon. She seems pleased, he satisfied, and my family discover how much half a day of my presence is worth.

Your letter finds me in the hospital, where I am shut in with the sunshine, and going to make a careful study of my health. Last Saturday, after an unusually busy week, I found myself exhausted. I am ashamed of being so tired. So I came down here to rest. The breath of Spring is all about me as I write, for the room is full of flowers sent by my "rosebud garden of girls"! Their constant thoughtfulness sweetens life at every step, and I feel rich in their love, whether it chances to find expression in roses and lilies or not.

And you want me to be with you? Well, I will be somewhere, some when, somehow. Only it can't be this vacation. But you are simply an old splendid to ask me. Give me advice about a new suit. I saw in Boston a dress of almost invisible green. It occurred to me it would be pretty for spring and fall days, with a bonnet of the same, brightened with a dash of color. One could wear with it creamy tea roses, or apple blossoms, or scarlet poppies in the fall. Kate says, "Your hair and eyes are just the same color. Get a dress to match." Annic thinks dark brown or deep wine color would be better. Now what do you, my artist, advise?

But I must stop. Annie will fill up the envelope. It makes me cough to write. I had a slight hemorrhage last week, and so must rest. Everybody — especially Mr. Durant and Miss Howard — is angelic. Mr. D. came and talked with me a long time on Thursday. He said, "You shall have two assistants next year. I'll do anything in the world if you'll only get well, Miss Freeman."

Since I found myself in the novel condition of being really ill two months ago, I have been in great doubt much of the time about what I ought to do. I need rest and quiet more than anything else. I have given up much of my extra work, and still have kept as much as possible. During these few days of pleasant weather I have grown better rapidly.

Dr. Bowditch, the authority on lung diseases in Boston, whom I consulted last week, told me that with great caution I might remain here awhile, unless I grow worse. It is very bad for the college and for me to give up now, unless continuing the responsibility is entirely unsafe. So I conclude to wait until the spring vacation. If then I do not feel equal to the next term's work, they offer leave of absence until September. The first two weeks in April I shall spend on the old farm in Southern New York, where I shall have fresh air and quiet to my heart's content. Through this rest I hope to be better than ever before.

So you see, sir, I am provided for and have no occasion to accept your generous offer. But I thank you for it. It will be something good to remember. In case of emergency I shall feel that I may go to you for advice and assistance. I cannot afford to break down now. There is so much to do before I can rightfully take the rest that I had hoped not to need for years yet. But I have been very foolish to overwork so here, and shall steadfastly refuse to do double work hereafter. Give my hearty good wishes to your wife and daughter.

I have succeeded in avoiding fresh colds and am charmed that I have had no drawbacks of any kind. Don't you people worry over my "going back." Miss Howard and I have the matter well in hand. She is delightful to me, and I am to have no further responsibility in the house. I have arranged for only five recitations and lectures a week next term. I shall not try to prove to any one that I have done more hard thinking in the last three years on the subject of my health — and to more purpose also — than they imagine. But my physicians know that I could not otherwise have rallied from the Saginaw experience.

It hurts me to have those I love fretted more than is necessary.

Mother, I never was in quite such perplexity before. Formerly when a teacher was sick, either in hospital or absent from College, the salary went on. Last summer the Trustees passed a law that when a teacher was away her salary should be stopped. Four of us have been overworked and have had to leave. We are all in the same situation, to us entirely unexpected. The policy may not be generous, considering how teachers work here; but there is nothing to be done. I am out of a month's salary, besides all the expense of medicine, doctors, and traveling. I am troubled, especially at not finding it out until so late. Mr. Durant is sick again, Miss Howard tired and away, and nothing is done on time in matters of business.

When I found this out yesterday, I wrote C., telling him I wanted fifty dollars of the hundred he owes me sent at once to F., that if he could n't send it all immediately, he must send what he could next week If he does this, and F. can spare fifteen of it to pay you what I borrowed, I shall be much relieved. If he does n't, F. must run in debt, and I will send enough to meet all the bills at the next payment the first of June. This being sick all winter has certainly taken two hundred dollars out of my pocket, and I am afraid it will be five hundred before all is ended. I am glad you were able to make that good investment; but don't put out any more at present, for I have set my heart on your coming East and Papa's visiting his relations in the West this summer. Fifty dollars apiece pays traveling expenses, and I am going to set apart that from my salary for May and June for this specific purpose. I don't want father to sell his horse and carriage so long as he stays in Saginaw. Work presses, and I stop.

Mr. Durant preached to-day. If only you could have heard him, all of you! It seems as if some great strange thing had happened, and we must speak and walk softly — as when some one has died. There was an atmosphere of sacredness about it all. It is enough to break one's heart to see his grand white head among these hundreds of girls, and hear him plead with them for "noble, white, unselfish womanhood;" to hear him tell of his hope and happiness in them, and his longing that "the blood of Jesus Christ should cleanse them from all sin." That was his text. I never heard and never shall hear anything quite like it for clear logic and tender appeal. This is the second time he has preached.

I heard a man at church this morning whose voice called back the dear old Windsor days. I wonder how the sermons which I used to think so good there would impress me now! This was a half hour of absolute commonplace. The man appeared to be a devoted soul who really wished to be useful, but who had n't an idea in his head of what people are thinking about. If such people would only buy farms and withdraw from trying to be leaders! Religious people now feel that they have no right to waste time in hearing pious nothings uttered by men who will not take the trouble to do any thinking. I fancy that nowadays many stay away from church conscientiously.

Last Tuesday everything passed off successfully, I believe; though I could not judge very well, as I had to stand at the reception-room door and "receive." But I did not enjoy the address. It does seem impossible for a man to come here and speak in a sensible way to sensible women. As usual, our orator talked in a superior way about woman's nature and condition, health, etc. He said he "knew the depths of a woman's heart." If I live a thousand years, I hope I may never make that remark about any man. I wait eagerly for the time when men will take our ability to study for granted, and will tell us what we want to hear about other subjects.

These are but trifles, dear mother, I send for your festival. Since I have only you for my little girl,

I lavish my playthings upon you. I had planned something different. But the truth is I am having a hard time to get through the year. Not that I am sick, but I am very busy with doing "last things," and very anxious about Mr. Durant's health. Just now I am writing my annual report for the Trustees' meeting next week. There are to be radical changes, some overturnings, and it is a question how some things will end. But I do not propose to worry.

And so it is your birthday, you bride-to-be! Here's a kiss for your forehead, and one for each of your blue eyes and sweet lips — even though they are now all another's. But on a birthday you belong especially to "the family." Happy may you be when you reach a birthday which doubles these years! It's so beautiful out in the future for you; the onward path looks so safe and sweet. God keep you always glad and warm in the loving arms, both heavenly and earthly! I had a letter to-night from that happy wife E., and ever since have been thinking how blessed a thing it is to be the centre and soul of a real home, always certain that a tender heart holds you close. That certainly includes all that is best in life.

As for myself I am beginning to get into the college a little more, and I like what I have exceedingly. But I don't feel at all satisfied with what I am doing nor with the distribution of my time. What with domestic work, corridor care, section meetings, and all the unexpected breaks that will come, I seem to accomplish very little; and there is so much of everything to be done here before things are as they ought to be! Perhaps each day's little doing counts. I hope so. One must be patient, and these girls are certainly beautiful.

This is so depressing a week that everything goes hard. We have just come from a meeting in the chapel, which is draped in the heaviest mourning. The desk on the platform has in front Garfield's picture, life size, surrounded by heavy black folds. All around the platform and gallery draperies of black and white are festooned. A large flag hangs at half-mast from the organ. But I can't make it seem possible that he is really dead. The students have had a mass meeting and nominated the president of each class as a committee to write a letter of sympathy to Mrs. Garfield. Last night the Faculty had a meeting and appointed me to write her also, expressing their united sorrow.

But we are in greater trouble over Mr. Durant than words can tell. He has been growing worse. Yesterday there was a council of four physicians from Boston and one from Philadelphia. Their decision was unanimous that there is little chance of recovery. They told Mrs. Durant; and when Mr.

Durant asked what they had said, she told him. In the afternoon, "in case he should become unconscious," he left his final instructions about the college — "Christ's College," he called it. All we can do now is to wait and carry on the college work.

All goes smoothly. Miss Howard has been in bed three days this week, and is not well at any time; nor have we enough teachers to meet the extra demands made by the new students. But my department is well organized, is running regularly, and it is understood that this year I do the work of only one. Several much-needed reforms in college arrangements have been brought about, reforms over which I have been very anxious. Altogether there is much that is hopeful in the outlook and my seven Ann Arbor friends here make the place a kind of home for me.

My dear Mrs. Freeman:

When Alice told me at the dinner table how busy she had been this morning and was likely to be this afternoon, I begged the privilege of writing her home-letter this week. She consented, on condition of my assuring you that she gives up the pleasant duty not because she is not well or does not long to do it, but simply because she has such a multitude of things to attend to. I may say that I have been happily surprised to find how good her health has been throughout this term. She has learned to take care of herself much better than formerly, and I am greatly encouraged. There seem to have been good reasons for her breaking down last Spring, which do not now exist, and I have much hope that she will keep well all the year.

You will not wonder at her finding no time to write to-day when I tell you the great news. At a meeting of the Executive Committee of the Board of Trustees held this morning, Miss Alice E. Freeman was appointed Vice-President of Wellesley College for the remainder of the year! Won't you be astonished? There will be astonishment here to-night when the announcement is made. I think nobody has a suspicion of the design of the Trustees, but I am equally sure that there will be universal delight. Alice herself had not a hint of the matter till Tuesday. She was undecided at first, and did not accept until she had talked the matter over with Miss Howard, Mrs. Durant, and the Executive Committee, so that there is a perfect understanding. She is wonderfully fitted for the place, which is virtually that of President. Miss Howard goes away at once for rest, leaving Alice in sole charge. You probably know that Miss Howard's health is still feeble. A good deal of the time she is unable to attend to the duties of her position. Alice is not to be subordinate to her, but equal except in name. The Trustees have said, "Do whatever you think best, Miss Freeman, and we will stand by you." She is to retain charge of the department of history, but is to have a second assistant and to meet no classes except the seniors, and them only twice a week during the second half of the year. She prefers to do a little teaching for the sake of contact with the girls.

Oh! I know she will succeed splendidly. Mr. Durant loved and trusted her perfectly. All the Trustees have entire confidence in her, and there is nobody else here whom the girls so universally admire and love. We Ann Arbor people are very proud. We are hoping Alice will not need to work harder than she has been working, though of course her responsibility will be much heavier. But she will have such hearty coöperation on all sides that I think she will not find the burden too great. I feel quite exalted to be the first to tell you of this honor, but you can hardly be prouder of Alice than you have already had reason to be.

(Later.) I wish Alice's father and mother could have been in the chapel to-night when, before evening prayers, the chairman of our Executive Committee made the announcement of her promotion. His words, so fervent and strong, were such as Mr. Durant himself might have used. To me it will always be a memorable occasion. But I must lose no time in sending off this letter with its great news. M. O. M.

I have been writing letters every moment to-day, none of them personal you may be sure, all on college business, and still I go to bed with twenty-three left for to-morrow. When I am fairly started in my new work I hope to keep more nearly even. To-morrow I am invited to lunch with one of the Trustees, and all are as kind and cordial as possible. The girls and teachers too are so loyal and thoughtful that I am full of hope, even though I can never see my way a single day ahead. There is a great deal in it all that is pleasant, but during the last two months I have been obliged to get a good many things — warm things for winter and a few nice things suitable for "the acting president." You see I have to wear good clothes all the time now to compensate for my undignified appearance. How much I would give for a few gray hairs! I am glad you are glad at the promotion, and that Saginaw people are pleased. Warm letters come from many friends.

VII

THE WELLESLEY PRESIDENCY

In speaking of Mrs. Palmer just after her death President Eliot said: "As we look back on the chief events of her too short career, the first thing that strikes us is its originality at every stage; she was in the best sense a pioneer all through her life. When she went to the University of Michigan as a student, she was one of a small band of young women, venturing with motives of intellectual ambition into a state university which had just been opened to women. At twenty-two years of age she was already principal of a high school in Michigan. At twenty-four she took a professorship of history in a new college for women where all the officers and teachers were women — a pioneer work indeed. At twenty-six she became president of that novel college, at a time when its worth had not yet been demonstrated. Indeed its policy was then held by many to be of doubtful soundness, and its financial future extremely difficult. What courage and devotion these successive acts required! Her work at Wellesley was creation, not imitation; and it was work done in the face of doubts, criticisms, and prophecies of evil."

How original Miss Freeman was at Wellesley becomes plainer when we consider how short a time she was there. Her administration lasted but six years. Beginning with the so-called vice-presidency in November, 1881, it ended in December, 1887. During this brief term Miss Freeman created a Wellesley type which has proved durable. This and the following chapters set forth the means by which this was accomplished. Briefly, it may be said that she fashioned the college after her own image. But what were her policies and methods? Where lay her difficulties? By what successive changes in organization, studies, finances, equipment, did she so suddenly transform a hastily gathered and somewhat distrusted body of teachers and pupils into the firm-built college which, when she left it, commanded universal respect? These questions can be answered only imperfectly, partly because of that very originality which lends a sort of mystery to all her doings, partly on account of the absence of early documents. In that confused time there were no financial statements, no records of the Faculty, no published reports of the president. Miss Freeman, it is true, at the close of her first year printed a president's report; but funds for the purpose seem to have been lacking, and the experiment was not repeated. Her letters seldom refer to her own affairs, but are full of those of the one to whom she writes. My acquaintance with either her or the college did not begin till near the close of her term. For the most part, therefore, I am obliged to depend on catalogues and on the memories of her early associates.

Pioneer as Miss Freeman was at Wellesley, her work there would have been impossible if the way had not been prepared by Mr. Durant. On his broad foundations she built. His large designs were hers also. He had selected her from the Faculty as the one whose temper was most congenial to his own. In the preceding chapter I have called attention to his dread of routine, his aversion to text-books, his approval of laboratory methods, original research, and whatever arouses individual activity. This forceful spirit shaped the plan of his college. In his catalogue for 1877 he announces that the conditions for entrance will be steadily raised. Then, after prescribing the studies of the freshman year, — and prescription was at that time the practice in all colleges except Harvard, — he proposes to throw open to sophomores seven different elective courses, or groups of studies, among which a student may choose. Each of these courses contains also within its coherent group large elements of election. And this is true even of that " general course " which he states is " for many probably the most desirable." Few colleges in the country had at that time a programme so liberal. He provides for graduate work, allows students not candidates for a degree to enter as specials, and offers to mature women who have been teaching for several years — "teacher specials" — the privilege of following for brief periods whatever studies they please. He encourages athletics too, introduces rowing, and requires of every girl at least an hour a day of exercise in the open air; declaring that "when the women of the country unite in observing, protesting against, and reforming the fatal causes which destroy girls' health, the calumny that woman's mind and woman's body are too frail to bear the pursuit of knowledge will perish with other forgotten prejudices."

In spite, however, of these far-sighted provisions, Wellesley College when Mr. Durant died was by no means what he or Miss Freeman desired it to be. In fact it existed but in germ. There had been no time to elaborate its organization. In the last two years Mr. Durant was sinking, as was also his lieutenant, Miss Howard; and in the previous years his own mind had passed through great changes in trying to grasp the notion of his proposed college. Originally he schemed it as a female seminary, after the pattern of Mt. Holyoke. For this a charter was obtained in 1870. In 1873 the name was changed to Wellesley College. In 1875 its vast building was opened and its first students were admitted. In 1877 the right to grant degrees was obtained. Not till 1879 did it graduate a class, or begin graduate work; not till 1880 did it drop its preparatory department. It was this rough sketch of a college, rather than the finished thing, which the girl-president received from the dying founder; a sketch truly noble, but needing correction, completion, and — as preliminary to these — a general setting in order. My presentation of her work at Wellesley will be divided into two parts: in the first I group her more important administrative measures, in the second I attempt some analysis of her personal influence.

Certain features of Mr. Durant's scheme, certain of its best features, were not developed. During Miss Freeman's administration the policy of elective studies was everywhere a novelty, and one which, being not yet understood, stirred strong opposition. It involved also grave financial difficulties in execution. It was an experimental method, which only a strong college could afford to practice extensively. Pressed upon a college not yet firmly organized, it tended to increase debt and disorder, its stimulating methods being easily mistaken for absence of restraint. Under election, too, more work is thrown on the Faculty, a class being broken up into small groups, each requiring a different treatment. More teachers are called for, and a larger fund for paying them than is necessary under the prescribed system. Wellesley was just starting. Its students, its teachers, were ill prepared for their strange work, and it had no endowment beyond grounds, buildings, and library. For such a college conservatism was wise. Naturally inclined by years and disposition to progressive methods, Miss Freeman on the whole held steadily to simplicity, order, solidity of organization, avoiding whatever might lead to confusion, looseness, experiment, and expense. Almost imperceptibly Mr. Durant's seven elective courses contracted themselves to two: the General Classical Course, leading to the B. A. degree — substantially as he had planned it — containing, besides its literature and history, a good dose of mathematics and science, a prescribed freshman year, and about a third of its later studies elective; while a course requiring no Greek at entrance, and having throughout a larger proportion of science, received the B. S. For music, as in Mr. Durant's time, no specific degree was given. A student was allowed to distribute music throughout either of the other two regular courses, thus expanding them to five years, and receiving a degree accordingly. Fuller development of the elective system was — in my judgment wisely — deferred to a later time. Nor can I learn that the three courses leading to advanced honors, which Mr. Durant planned, were ever considerably elected. Probably in that early day few students were suitably prepared.

But if Miss Freeman accepted a policy of restraint in the matter of election and did not carry individual option much beyond the point where Mr. Durant left it, she did so only in order that she might the more thoroughly consolidate instruction, adjust it to her limited means, and give the college a firmer hold on the community. The conditions for entrance were repeatedly raised and their exact enforcement watched. Greek was first required at entrance in 1881. English literature and composition were soon after added, with history, both ancient and modern. Special students were not admitted unless able to pass examinations. Greater care was used in setting and marking examination papers. In 1880 it had been decided to accept the certificates of certain schools as entitling their graduates to enter college without examination. This system has many advantages; but if the schools are not frequently inspected and held to a rigid standard, certification becomes a paper requirement and scholarship sinks. Miss Freeman systematized inspection and drew up a certificate which, while laying little stress on opinions about the student's competence, demanded the precise facts of her training during the immediately preceding years. Similar care in the conduct of examinations was enforced throughout the college. There was a general rise in standards. Many informants tell me that the most marked change produced by Miss Freeman's coming was this new atmosphere of exactitude, work, and insistence on what a college should mean, succeeding a sort of boarding-school looseness. The girls no longer played at going to college, — they really went.

How to obtain properly qualified students was a difficult problem. College-fitting schools for boys had long been common and excellent, but of course there could be nothing of the kind for girls until girls' colleges also came into being. In only a few high schools were girls allowed to join classes which fitted boys for college. On account of this lack of schools Mr. Durant was obliged to open a preparatory department and train his candidates from the start. For several years these students largely outnumbered those in the college. But in the year that Miss Freeman became vice-president the preparatory department was cut off and the independent fitting school of Dana Hall was established in Wellesley. To founding more such feeders Miss Freeman addressed herself, and her work in this direction was one of her greatest services to the college. In 1884 an important auxiliary school was opened in Philadelphia. Before the end of her presidency she had organized fifteen others in different parts of the country, officered for the most part by Wellesley graduates, and with courses so shaped by the college that their graduates could safely enter it on certificate. Perhaps this plan of connecting her college with a special group of schools was suggested to her by the example of Michigan.

One of Miss Freeman's chief anxieties was the problem of housing. To it she refers in her first report, and it never ceased to trouble her. Only so many students could be received as college buildings would hold; for the village of Wellesley, half a mile distant, was small and at that time ill provided with boarding-houses. On account of scanty accommodations more than a hundred desirable candidates were turned away each year. Indeed the number of students increased less than two hundred during the whole of Miss Freeman's presidency, rising gradually from four hundred and fifty to six hundred and twenty-five, as places for them could be found. The original building, four hundred and seventy-five feet long, held three hundred; Stone Hall, given by Mrs. Stone in 1880, taking another hundred. In 1881 Mr. Simpson gave a cottage with accommodations for twenty-five, and in the same year Mr. and Mrs. Durant fitted up a second cottage for half as many more. But when all were filled girls still clamored for entrance, and larger numbers would have benefited the college itself. While every college is in large measure a charity school and does not expect its students to pay for what they get, up to a limit this loss diminishes as students increase. A certain cost for plant is incurred in any case, and this may with advantage be widely distributed. While Miss Freeman had no financial responsibility — all funds being under the exclusive control of Mrs. Durant — she was naturally anxious to make the income more nearly equal the expense and also to extend the influence of Wellesley.

In 1885, when the decennial of the college arrived, she started a general subscription for a new hall, Norumbega, which was opened in the following year. But it was one of the disappointments of her administration that the public could not be brought at once to the support of Wellesley. Few gifts came from outside the circle of Mr. Durant's friends, though within that circle there were generous and discriminating givers. Professor Eben Norton Horsford, in particular, endowed the library, provided the means for granting professors sabbatical years, and in general looked after the comfort of students, teachers, and president with singular tact and devotion. But a larger income was necessary; and Miss Freeman, though feeling it well to keep the charges as low as possible and so to make the college accessible to poor students, was compelled to raise the fee for board and tuition in 1882 from two hundred and fifty dollars to two hundred and seventy-five, and again in 1884 to three hundred. Aids to students, however, were also increased. In her presidency the number of scholarships was doubled, as were too the gifts of the Students' Aid Society, a band of ladies organized for the private assistance of those in need. To commemorate Miss Freeman after she became Mrs. Palmer, Mrs. Durant in 1888 erected a new hall and named it Freeman Cottage.

But if Miss Freeman was thus hampered by the inadequate preparation of students and by meagre financial resources, she became only the more determined and ingenious in providing her girls the utmost still possible in scholarship, health, character, and enjoyment. Where little money is, there often appears a kind of compensatory devotion. Perhaps too the limitation of numbers was for another reason not altogether a loss. It enabled her to choose from those who applied the intellectually and physically strong, giving her a compact body of earnest students who counted themselves exceptionally fortunate. Such a company is excellent material for the building of a college. In it hard work, loyalty, unity of ideals are more easily secured. All students of that day knew one another's names and were known by their president. Friendships were more intimate, the life of the college more intense, romance was easy.

As regards teachers Miss Freeman's policy was to spend on them the largest possible percentage of income. She wished to see their number increase and their hours of work diminish. She herself had

had serious experience in the debilitating effects of many required hours. She knew that the most stimulating teaching cannot be had from those who lack leisure. Of course salaries were small; but she contrived to secure half a dozen capital scholars in her chief chairs and to assure herself that each person appointed to an inferior post had some distinctive merit. She understood that the deepest claim on her as an appointer came from the students, that they be assured of excellent teaching; and that the claim of individual teachers was only secondary, that they be kept in comfortable places. She did not hesitate therefore kindly to drop a tolerable instructor so soon as a superior appeared. Her estimate of persons was pretty accurate, and she left a much stronger Faculty than she found.

That Faculty was built up out of departmental groups, that is, all teachers dealing with a common subject were banded together under a head-professor and constituted a single unit. This professor arranged the work of the department and was responsible for its quality to the president. Miss Freeman developed and dignified the departments. They appear for the first time in her second catalogue, their organized meetings beginning in the preceding year. They then numbered twelve, but had risen to sixteen when she retired. In earlier days teachers of every rank met in the not very important faculty meetings, to discuss such details of government or instruction as were not already settled by Mr. Durant. After the formation of departments Miss Freeman left to the general Faculty matters of discipline and of routine administration, but more and more turned to the heads of departments for consultation on questions of educational policy. In this way almost insensibly there grew up the body known as the Academic Council, which has continued to this day. Seeking stability as she everywhere did, she found she could best send her ideas through the college by coming close to the permanent leaders. For similar reasons, standing committees were formed to take charge of such weighty interests as entrance examinations, preparatory schools, graduate instruction, the library, the choice of studies; this last committee being a veritable board of advisers, to which every girl must submit her schedule of electives before she could register it as her own.

The library had its collections doubled and its cataloguing systematized. Much was done for the laboratories, for which she makes an appeal in her first report. She refitted the gymnasium, introducing into it the Sargent system of apparatus, of measurements, and health records, and putting at its head an enthusiastic director of physical culture. Competitive contests were forbidden, but such coöperative sports as bring health, enjoyment, and grace were earnestly encouraged. Attention was paid to the voices of the students, and an officer was appointed to train them in quiet and expressive reading. Ventilation and hygiene were insisted on. During her time the college passed through no serious illness. Perhaps she took more care of the health of the students through being herself a physician's daughter.

Providing thus for the internal well-being of the college, she soon began to study its relations with the outside world. In those days Wellesley was more isolated than at present. Its charming hills and woods were little known. Mr. and Mrs. Durant had loved modesty more than advertising, and their college came into existence without that noise which has latterly been thought appropriate to the birth of universities. So quiet an infancy pleased Miss Freeman; but as the college grew, she resolved to bring it into closer connection with other colleges and with the community around. This attempt made one of the distinctive features of her administration. Of course her attractive personality and winning speech opened all doors, and in the interest of Wellesley she accepted invitations for public addresses up to the limits of her strength. In different parts of the country she helped to found Wellesley clubs. To Wellesley she invited whatever notable person visited the neighboring cities. In her last year more than fifty public lectures were given there, and half as many concerts. Only one vacancy occurred in the Board of Trustees in her time, but she reconstituted the subordinate board, the Board of Visitors, and packed it with experts, who brought criticism and encouragement to the various departments. To enlarge the social life of teachers and students, she held frequent receptions and introduced to Wellesley the men and women of Cambridge and Boston. Into the society of those cities she herself entered. From Harvard she sometimes borrowed temporary teachers and with that university she soon established relations which a certain dislike on Mr. Durant's part for his *alma mater* had prevented from being earlier formed.

Such then were some of the constructive methods by which a scholarly, united, and admired college was rapidly built up. Seeking to raise the rank of Wellesley until it should equal that of any New England college, she found herself hampered by lack of fitting schools, by a loose system of admission on certificate, by lack of accommodation in college buildings for suitable numbers, and by consequent lack of funds. She found her teachers too few, badly chosen and badly paid, burdened with excessive routine work, and needing to be more solidly organized into departments. She found meagre laboratories and library, no provision for physical training, and little connection between the college and the learned and social world outside. At the close of her administration these deficiencies had disappeared, without leaving debt behind.

This truly creative work was accomplished by substantially the methods here described. There is nothing striking about them. They cannot be turned into attractive reading. Hearing of Miss Freeman's brilliant administration, we do not naturally think of measures so homespun and painstaking. For that reason I have lingered long on this first part of my account, trying to explain the dry professional technicalities over which her young years were spent. But I imagine most of us will hardly be interested in watching the work of an architect's office. The result alone engages us. All beauty, however, is grounded in such technicalities, and originality consists in finding the beauty there. That at least was the type of her originality. She was no revolutionist, but out of almost any humdrum and disheartening conditions she would contrive to evolve life. Or do I wrong her in speaking of contrivance? Was it rather that her believing and creative mind saw nothing of what others counted humdrum and disheartening, being altogether occupied with the ideal hid within? It may be so. She took her duties lightly and once exclaimed to the president of another college, "Is n't it fun to be a president!" When I applied to her faithful secretary for information about the perplexities of these opening years, I received the following reply: "The thought of Miss Freeman's feeling any perplexity in her position at Wellesley seems strange to me, who knew so well the inner life of the office. Underneath her cheerfulness, her keen sense of humor, her thoughtfulness for others, her joy in all that makes life lovely, there ran a current of confidence and unhesitating trust in her Heavenly Father. She consequently never appeared perplexed. The presidency of Wellesley was not a difficult position for her. In each emergency she saw by intuition the right course to pursue." But that she, almost the first of woman presidents and with little in the past for a guide, should have possessed this instinctive discernment and, youthful and ardent though she was, should have known that it is the plodding path which leads to glory, must, I suppose, indicate in her something like genius.

Academic Portrait

VIII

THE WELLESLEY PRESIDENCY (CONTINUED)

THE account of Miss Freeman's career at Wellesley thus far given is obviously unfair and incomplete: unfair because it assumes that the policies described were altogether hers, regardless of the wise and loyal coöperation of her fellow trustees and professors. Yet this unfairness is so inevitable that it will readily be pardoned. We are obliged to say that Wellington won Waterloo, though we know how helpless he would have been without the courage of the undistinguished soldier. Miss Freeman always declared that the rapid rise of Wellesley was due to a multitude of causes and persons. Of course it was, a multitude directed by herself. No president ever had better helpers; nor they, one whom it was better worth while to help.

But in calling my account incomplete I speak of something of larger consequence, and to repairing the omission I devote this entire chapter; for the administrative measures just recounted could have had no such effect as actually followed if they had not been supported throughout by an extraordinary personal influence. Personality and policies together composed Miss Freeman's power, spirituality and mechanics, the two supplemental, each of little worth without the other. To considering some aspects of that pervasive personal influence I now turn.

In the first place Miss Freeman came into very close contact with her students. She lived among them, until her last year having her private rooms in immediate connection with her business offices in the great building. Even when she removed to quieter quarters in Norumbega Cottage, she dined every day with thirty girls and talked with double that number. Each morning she held office hours, when any student could consult her on any subject. But she did not shut her door at other times, and a large part of every day was given to these interviews. In that small office the bent of many a life has been determined. At that time there was no dean. All the care of the students fell upon her. By some means she managed to meet most of them soon after their arrival and to turn their faces in the right direction. It was done incidentally, with few words, and quite as a matter of course. A student writes:—

"When I entered Wellesley, I arrived late in the afternoon and was shown to my room. Soon a bell rang, and I tried to find the dining room. I went down to the first floor and wandered to the south door. There, by good luck, stood Miss Freeman, looking out over the lake. Of course she came to me at once, asked who I was, said the college would be good to me, and then took me to the dining room, talking in her easy cordial fashion all the way, and found a place for me at one of the tables. I wish I could remember the things she said. I only recall the strong impression of her kindness."

When a girl had once been spoken to, however briefly, her face and name were fixed on a memory where each incident of her subsequent career found its place beside the original record. A superintendent of education sends me the following instance: —

"Once after she had been speaking in my city, she asked me to stand beside her at a reception. As the Wellesley graduates came forward to greet her — there were about eighty of them — she said something to each which showed that she knew her. Some she called by their first names; others she asked about their work, their families, or whether they had succeeded in plans about which they had evidently consulted her. The looks of pleased surprise which flashed over the faces of those girls I cannot forget. They revealed to me something of Miss Freeman's rich and radiant life. For though she seemed unconscious of doing anything unusual, and for her I suppose it was usual, her own face reflected the happiness of the girls and showed a serene joy in creating that happiness."

Probably she had a natural aptitude for such remembrance, but she cultivated it also. An eminent journalist writes: "I recall a memorable conversation I once had with her. She had told me a little of the means she took in getting and keeping in mind the names of her many hundred Wellesley girls, and I said, 'That is something I never could do.' 'Oh yes, you could,' she replied, 'if you had to. It is simply that you never had to do it. Whatever we have to do we can always do.' This quiet confidence in the ability to do what needs to be done seems to me one of the secrets of her power. She leaned on her necessities, instead of letting herself be broken by them; and that simple disclosure of her method has greatly added to the power of my life."

But in her close contact with students, playful though it often was, she kept her dignity and her easy power of command. In a previous chapter I have shown how important for the young college was the almost despotic control exercised by Mr. Durant. This she inherited, and in her own way maintained. She tempered it, it is true, with singular sweetness, usually capturing love and approval before obedience. But nevertheless, her will was law. Trustees, Faculty, and students alike gave it a pretty free course. All felt in her what Kent saw in Lear: "You have that in your countenance which I would fain call master." This was well understood and, becoming a tradition, tended to perpetuate itself. A gentleman tells me that when he attended a small New England College he found some of the regulations galling. On remonstrating he was told, "You had better go to Wellesley, where, whenever the little president raises her hand, the whole college hurries to obey." Yet her authority did not rest on bare will; on knowledge rather, on sanity, poise, and a large way of handling business.

> An incidental greatness charactered
> Her unconsidered ways.

An instructive anecdote has been sent me: "There came to Wellesley for a period of special study a woman who had already spent several years in teaching. She was nervous, vain, and touchy, easily finding in whatever was said or looked some covert disparagement of herself. As she was complaining one day of some recent rudeness, Miss Freeman said, 'Why not be superior to these things and let them go unregarded? You will soon find you have nothing to regard.' 'Miss Freeman,' retorted Miss S., 'I wonder how *you* would like to be insulted.' Miss Freeman drew herself up with splendid dignity: 'Miss S., there is no one living who *could* insult me.' And she was right. Nobody would have dared do so. But had they attempted it, they would have found her altogether beyond their reach."

I cannot discover that the universal worship marred in any respect her simplicity or transferred her attention from the matter in hand to herself. She took it lightly, as a part of the nature of things. Love was inherently good, and people should practice it. I think she would have been disturbed by its absence. Being given, she did not dwell upon it as due to herself, but chiefly noticed the new worth it gave the giver. Nobody could claim love as by right. I have often heard her quote George Herbert's noble line, —

> Love is a present for a mighty king.

When she came upon a specific case of adoration it humbled her.

Having, then, such intimacy with the students and at the same time such exaltation above them, she was in the best position to call on them for aid in any exigency. And this she constantly did, letting them understand that the college depended on them for its well-being, and that they were to coöperate with her in keeping it sound. Nobody was allowed to forget its great motto. One writes: "During my last winter an epidemic of hysteria seized the college, chiefly the freshmen. There were frequent screams over trifles, and gossip ran riot. Miss Freeman called us seniors together and said she held us responsible for the continuance of such folly. What did we older girls mean by allowing an atmosphere where such things were possible? It stopped."

Or again: "An incident showed me how she kept individual students in mind and heart. There came to college from my city an eccentric, lawless girl, J. L. Before her lawlessness was fully known Miss Freeman was much concerned about her, hearing (she always did hear or see everything) that J. was ostracized and unhappy. There were many Kentucky girls in college then, but I was the oldest of them. Miss Freeman accordingly sent for me, told me frankly that she was worried about J.'s future, and said that if she was to be made into a worthy student the girls must help. She asked me to bring the other Kentucky girls into friendly relations with J. and try to change her attitude. We did try, but it was useless. J. was an anarchist from birth, and soon left college."

One morning she announced at prayers that she had turned " some girl " out of college, and did n't wish to hear of her again. Lately, when silly rumors had been flying about the grounds and she had asked students where they got them, they had said, "Some girl told me." That girl was gone. Hereafter they need n't believe anything they heard from a person without a name. One winter an attempt was made to blackmail an important person connected with the college. Because it was bravely resisted, serious scandal was threatened. Before the papers spoke, Miss Freeman called her girls together, told them briefly the dastardly story, declared it false, and said she should rely on them to refuse to speak of it either among themselves or to others. The newspapers thundered, but Wellesley noticed nothing. It was strangely absorbed in its own pursuits.

This coöperative method was even applied to the single student. When a girl brought her a request which she could not grant, she seldom gave it an immediate refusal; she set before her petitioner the considerations involved, obliged her to do her own thinking, and finally to suggest as of herself the very settlement which Miss Freeman approved. Amusing stories are reported of girls who came to ask for something, and went away delighted to have obtained the opposite.

One of them says: "In the spring of my senior year I had an invitation to spend the holidays in Washington, and my family strongly urged me to arrange the visit. Overjoyed, I went to Miss Freeman to obtain permission to leave college several days before the vacation. She was very warm, envying me the prospect of seeing the Capitol for the first time. She promised to ask the Faculty for permission and to state to them how great the opportunity for me was. But she inquired how many examinations and written exercises I should miss, incidentally calling attention to the fact that the professors would have to give me special ones in the following term. Gradually I felt the disadvantage of this irregularity. Still, there was Washington! And I asked if she herself would not be tempted to go? Indeed she would, she said, but college work was the nearest, the first, business. A Washington invitation might come again; a senior year in college, never. So, quite as if my own judgment had been my guide, I decided that I did not want to go to Washington. A little later, when the office door had closed, I stopped on the stairs and asked myself if this was the same person who had passed there half an hour before, and what had induced me to give up the coveted journey when there was no hint on Miss Freeman's part of compulsion, much less of refusal."

College presidents are sometimes suspected by students of prevarication and falsehood, and certainly they are often called on to look at the same subject from different points of view. But her girls knew that though she might guide them skilfully, she persistently sought their interest. Her heart was with them. She was an obstinate believer in their worth. In later life, as we walked the streets of a foreign city, she would often be seized in passing by some exclamatory girl; and when after too long delay I disengaged her and asked who this tiresome person was, she pretty regularly answered, "Why, don't you know Mary X? She was one of the most remarkable girls we ever graduated from Wellesley." They all were, and the hardy faith carried both her and them through many difficulties. One of them shall describe the process:—

"A great reason for her strange control of girls was, I think, that she always seized on some good point in a girl's character, emphasized that, and made the girl feel that she must bring the whole up to the level of this. She took for granted, or appeared to do so, the girl's good intentions. Many a time I have heard her say with the greatest apparent confidence to some wavering girl, 'Of course you could n't do anything in this matter that is untrue or unladylike. That would be quite out of keeping with you.' And the wavering girl was promptly strengthened in her determination to do the right thing at any cost. The same method was worked in intellectual ways. My friend Miss M. returned to Wellesley after a four years' absence, hoping to complete her course in a year. The advanced requirements made this difficult. She talked over the situation with Miss Freeman, feeling greatly discouraged before the interview. Miss Freeman sketched out the hard necessary work and said, 'Now, Miss M., that is what I call a stiff schedule; but with your habits it is possible enough.' Miss M. went out determined not to disappoint her confidence, and she did not."

Sometimes there was no direct appeal to a better nature in the one who sought her aid, but a kind of transmission of force occurred through mere contact. Virtue went out from her. In a letter received shortly after her death I read:—

"Mrs. Palmer had a strange effect on me. When I saw her, I felt as if I could do things that I never dreamed of before. Even now, whenever I think of her, I have a sense of dignity in my life. I don't know what it is. It seems as if her appreciation of the worth of things puts a spirit into me that carries me along until the next time I think of her. I should n't care to go on in a world in which she had n't been."

Probably the ennobling atmosphere which seemed thus to radiate from her presence was in some measure connected with her religious faith. She believed that conscious fellowship with God is the foundation of every strong life, the natural source from which all must derive their power and their peace. Hers was a dedicated soul. Mr. Durant had given the religious tone to Wellesley. This she deepened, diversified, and freed from artificiality. In the first year of her presidency she reformed the methods of Bible study, abolishing the daily classes to which no serious study was given, and which seemed to her to encourage sentimentality. Instead, she put into each year of the curriculum two hours a week of examinable instruction. She organized a Christian Association at

Wellesley, but refused to allow it to become affiliated with organizations elsewhere, or to be patterned after any narrow type. She turned it into a veritable college church, gathering into it devout souls of all sorts, and those who longed to be devout, until its ample organization embodied pretty fully the spiritual aspirations of the place. To it she transferred her own membership, and for the remainder of her life she belonged to no other church.

I am not aware that she ever conducted chapel services on Sunday, though she exercised much care in selecting those who did. But every morning she became the priestess of her household, regularly taking charge of prayers, and delighting so to begin the day. Attendance was then required. I doubt if one student less would have been present had there been no requisition. For all knew that prayer was her supreme expression; they felt the solemn glow and entered with her into a divine presence. Her voice throbbed with ardor, insight, and self-effacement. In simple language she spoke to God as one who had known God; and of her girls as one who understood their dreams, joys, and perplexities. I have observed that persons naturally reserved sometimes express their inmost minds more easily in public than in private. They are sheltered by the multitude. It was so with her, who rarely referred to religion in conversation. Her needy company set her free. All felt her love and genuineness, and wondered at the appropriateness of her words. It was commonly believed that Miss Freeman's Bible was not the ordinary volume, for out of it came strange chapters, extraordinarily fitted to whatever occasion arose. Her familiarity with it was large, and from that storehouse of spiritual experience she liked to bring together passages from writers of different times uttering a similar thought in unlike ways. The morning assembly, too, she found a convenient occasion for addressing the whole body of students on matters of general consequence.

But there is danger in the religious temper. For some persons the light of eternal things casts a shade over the temporal. In view of what is abiding and august, the passing interest is dulled. This danger even besets those who are predominantly moral. They become narrow, heedless of what cannot at once be related to law; while momentary matters, chance, facts, the mere happenings of our hurly-burly world, do not joyously engage them. This is the same as to say that such persons frequently lack humor and spontaneity — yes, strongly marked individuality. Of course deficiencies quite as grave are noticeable in those who follow their own vagrant will and listen to the call of the instant. They are soon found unimportant in the stress of serious affairs. Yet their temperament forms a necessary supplement to the profounder insights of the austere. A saintly minister of my acquaintance on being asked why he was going to Europe for the summer, wisely answered, "To de-moralize myself." We queer human creatures cannot fill out our full stature till we harmonize within us contradictory attributes.

Such splendid contradictions shone in Miss Freeman, giving her access to persons of every type and imparting to herself perpetual freshness. Custom never staled her. It easily might, had not she been she; for she was called to set a woman's college in order. I have shown how her administration tended everywhere to solidity and respect for law; how she herself was a prodigious force for righteousness among her girls. Yet this seriousness was but one aspect of her, and must straightway be offset in any just estimate of her influence. For hers was essentially a spontaneous and abounding nature. She found her way to an important issue as often blindly as through calculation. One cannot say too often how impulsive she was, sportive, enchanted with the shifting show, the swiftly varying expressions of her face telling how eagerly she followed the flight of things that cannot endure. One writes: "I doubt if I ever knew any one who gave me so strong a feeling of the pure joy of living." It was as good as a circus to be with her, for something novel was always going on. And this incessant regard for the small and momentary was treated as altogether honorable, in herself or in another. She was no dualist, no separator of sacred and profane, of petty and profound. All had significance and found their fitting place in her responsive soul. "One flower, one tree, one baby, one bird singing, or one little village would move her to love and praise as surely as a garden, a forest, a university, an orchestra, or a great city." I never knew one who more fully, with William Blake,

> Could see a world in a grain of sand,
> And a heaven in a wild flower;
> Hold infinity in the palm of the hand,
> And eternity in an hour.

Or with one of her own favorite poets, Henry Vaughan, could so —

> Feel through all this fleshly dress
> Bright shoots of everlastingness.

Such exuberant many-sided life was of peculiar consequence in the work to which she was called. It was hers to set the pattern of a woman president of a woman's college. In private life we prize woman not merely for her priestly qualities, but quite as much for her vivacity, swiftness of perception, ease in being pleased, and interested acceptance of what each moment brings. Should these fascinating features of traditional womanhood be retained on her entrance into official life, or should they be crowded out by the proprieties, decorums, and conformities to which woman is also prone? Alice Freeman showed which is the more admirable, which the more influential too. She never sank her own variable personality in the great official. She kept the child-like in the larger mind. By thus remaining truly a woman she protected womanliness among her students. Through her, freedom and naturalness pervaded Wellesley. Bounteously original herself, she fostered whatever special quality those about her possessed and taught it to come forth with grace and helpfulness. Girls are easily crushed or starved. Nowhere is wealth of nature more important than in their leader. Perhaps, too, respect for temperamental differences was not at that time so generally practised as it happily is now.

Obviously, however, a great personality cannot be cut up into sections and listed. I may seem to have attempted something of the sort in successively setting down these modes of her personal influence. But that would be to disintegrate and falsify one who through all her variety was always the same beautiful whole. All I have desired is to trace a few of the channels through which that curious influence ran. Thus I have shown in what close contact with her girls she lived, though preserving always her distinction and her power of instantaneous command; how she summoned them to coöperate with her, made them feel that it was their college no less than hers, and called on them to keep it vigorous and sweet; how in dealing with individuals she paid attention to whatever was excellent in them and let the poorer parts pretty much alone; how she treated them all as children of God who longed for a fuller embodiment of Him in their daily lives; how she even respected spontaneous nature and did not in the interest of a strained spirituality repress the happy waywardness of herself or her girls. But I am not so simple as to suppose that by this summary I have explained her, or that the methods here toilsomely enumerated can be codified in the next handbook of pedagogics and used by any newly elected president. Properly speaking, these are not methods at all. They are merely her ways, the natural expressions of a unique human being who was not afraid of herself or of obstacles, but ruled, loved, planned, enjoyed, and builded as best she could, with little help from past experience and with little consciousness of doing anything remarkable. Just nine years after she entered the university as a student she became president. When she retired, after her extraordinary, brief, but durable success, she was only a little older than the youngest college president who has ever taken office elsewhere. The mysterious power of characterful youth had more than counterbalanced the deficient age. Long ago Isaiah remarked that "a child may die an hundred years old; but the sinner being an hundred years old shall be accursed."

In this analysis of her work at Wellesley I have not paused to relate events of her own life. In reality there were none. Her life was merged in that of the college. One of her days was much like another. At Norumbega she took breakfast in her room, selecting then the hymn and Scripture for the day. Prayers followed at 8.30. Afterwards she attended to her mail and held office hours for consultation with students. These were usually prolonged through the morning, so that she rarely returned to her rooms at noon, unless to bring visitors, but took her luncheon in the main building. Afternoons were occupied with letters, callers, inspection of grounds, buildings, or departments, with interviews with teachers and parents, or with yet more students. Time too must be found for the occasional meetings of Trustees and Faculty, for seeing people in Boston, or for a public address. She tried to dine at home. When she did, she threw off all care and devoted herself more to the girls at her table than to her food, telling amusing stories and inciting those still better. After dinner she would take part in the merriment which usually preceded study hours. But quite as often she was unable to return to Norumbega till ten or eleven at night. Then she took a light lunch, read a while, — by preference poetry, — and was soon in bed. She was always a sound sleeper, and more dependent on sleep than food.

Twice a year she tried to visit her parents in Michigan, and usually succeeded in giving them a few weeks. But having no dean to represent her at Wellesley, she was much confined there and throughout her presidency took only one considerable vacation. This was in 1884. In that year an important International Conference on Education was held in London, to which she was appointed one of three American delegates. She had become much exhausted with work, and was advised that a voyage would invigorate her. In company with her father she saw England for the first time, addressing the Conference in a speech which Henry Sidgwick pronounced the best given there (Life and Letters, p. 384), and afterwards spending a few restful weeks at the English Lakes. In all, she was absent from Wellesley two months.

In 1887 Columbia University, in New York City, at its centennial celebration, conferred on her the degree of Doctor of Letters; Union University, at its centennial in 1896, that of Doctor of Laws. She became a Doctor of Philosophy at Michigan in 1882. Since her death, in recognition of the work described in this chapter, Wellesley graduates have endowed their presidency with a fund which bears her name.

I add a few letters which have been sent me in further illustration of her Wellesley ways.

LETTERS

It is impossible for the girls of later days, of more perfect organization and more divided responsibility, to realize how in that early time the whole college depended on this one personality. What she thought and said and did was the heart and centre of what the college thought and said and did. It would have been dangerous for one person to have so much power had not that person been Miss Freeman. What she was is best proved by what the place became. Through her administration Wellesley developed into a fully equipped college, thoroughly organized and efficiently conducted, known to all the world. However much the Wellesley ideal may have grown through longer experience and wider opportunities, we shall always owe to Miss Freeman the establishment of the type.

How she worked that year of her vice-presidency! Her interest in her own special department, that of history, could not be given up. She had planned a course for those brought that year to the college — teacher specials — and she must see it through; and she did. But how she toiled to conquer those old girls' diffidence, their previous lack of any and every training! How she labored to wake them up to possibilities of study and research! How she strove to impart to them her zeal and enthusiasm!

Her memory for names and faces was phenomenal. On my second visit to her office I volunteered my name and was met with the quick response, "Yes, I know." It was said that by the end of the first week of the college year she knew every one of her girls by name, and it was a pleasure to her to recognize them at all times, within doors or without.

So blind she was to our shortcomings, so unerring in finding the good that was in us! Gentle, womanly, responsive, and enthusiastic, with a genius for friendship and affection, she has sent uncounted numbers of us from her presence inspired to do the thing which was at the highest limit of our powers. It was her unshakable belief in the best side of our natures that made her optimism inspiring. In the heat of her intense idealism every objecting, hindering doubt was fused into a passion to do the work she knew we could do. Who of us will ever forget that flexible and endearing voice, or the beauty which poured from her smile, look, and gesture?

I had never been away from home until I went to Wellesley, and I was desperately homesick. At noon the second day I wandered after luncheon into the centre and sat down on a stair by the palms. I wanted to die. Just then a troop of people came toward me in animated talk. One of them, a lady young and beautiful, was speaking most eagerly. As they passed me, she, without pausing in what she was saying, turned and poured her kind eyes right into mine. I felt a new life come in. It would be good to be anywhere, I thought, if she were there. The next morning I went to chapel. She was at the desk. I whispered to my neighbor and learned that it was the president. I was not homesick again.

On my way to Wellesley for the first time I put myself under the care of Professor C. and went to the college with her. She took me to her own sitting-room, which she shared with Miss Freeman. The burst of welcome from Miss Freeman for her friend was irresistible and brought tears to my eyes. After the first greetings were over, Miss Freeman turned in her bright impulsive way to the little stranger, drew me into the circle, and began to help me off with my wraps. From the conversation, I gathered that she had not been well enough to "go on" for a classmate's wedding and was eager to hear an account of it from Miss C. But this did not check her service to me. I was taken to her own bedroom, given fresh towels, and cared for in every way. It was such a gracious thing, that welcome of Miss Freeman at such a time to a little stranger who might so easily have been turned over to others! The rest of the time I was at Wellesley (I left the following November, from illness) I saw Miss Freeman only at rare intervals. That one brief, bright glimpse is my permanent remembrance of her.

At one of the Faculty meetings in the first years of her presidency, when some grave academic questions were being discussed without much prospect of being brought to a conclusion, Miss Freeman was called to the door and found there the housekeeper of Dana Hall, who had insisted on seeing Miss Freeman. She had a carriage waiting to take her to Dana Hall to see the dress rehearsal of a French comedy which was soon to be given. The humor of the situation struck Miss Freeman. Returning to the room, she announced to the assembled professors that she had been called away on pressing business for an hour, and requested one of them to take the chair. Gleefully she drove to Dana Hall, flashed in at the performance, laughed steadily for half an hour, and came back to the tired Faculty, blithe and breezy, to swing the discussion on to a prompt conclusion.

Miss Freeman gave a series of talks to us seniors who intended to teach. They were frank discussions of the problems we should encounter and the right ways of meeting them. Nowadays they would probably be "pedagogy;" then they were simply "talks." She always tried to show both sides of a picture. On one occasion she told of a letter she had just received from the head of a school, asking for a new teacher. The former one had broken her contract and left her position in the middle of the year, in order to be married. After condemning the lack of honor shown, and saying it was a case where "woman's citadel, her affections, became her weakness," she went on to speak of the requirements demanded of the new candidate: she must be pleasing in person, highly trained intellectually, socially and morally an all-round example to her students, and would have a salary of $600. "I wrote the man," she said, "that at present we have no six-hundred-dollar angel."

When ill tidings came to a fellow student it eased the aching hearts of her friends to know that Miss Freeman had gone to her. And when it fell to the president to report a piece of good fortune, one girl, I am sure, will never forget the hearty handshake and evident feeling with which she said, "I wanted to tell you myself how glad I am for you."

That indefinable quality called "magnetism' was in all her public utterances. People listened spellbound, variously ascribing their interest to her charm of manner or her brilliancy in command of language. She never permitted the daily chapel exercise to become irksome or distasteful. It meant much to her personally, and she made it much to those who listened. There are hymns which many old Wellesley girls never read or sing but the remembrance of Miss Freeman comes to them. The tenderness of the first epistle of John has ever meant more to them because she read from it so lovingly. Her simple, earnest words of prayer went through the day's hard work and smoothed its perplexities. If she were absent from morning prayers, there was distinct disappointment. And following from day to day the varied petitions which suited the needs of this large body of students, one wondered that no stereotyped phrases or even repetitions came from her lips.

The portrait in the art gallery at Wellesley, ideally beautiful as it surely is, does not satisfy the old girls; it falls inevitably short of the remembrance of her, cherished for many years.

The full-length portrait of Mrs. Palmer by Abbott Thayer, which Professor Horsford presented to Wellesley in 1890, embodies a beautiful ideal of purely womanly womanhood. The painting might be prized as a picture of the eternal feminine, and evidently was painted as such *con amore* by the artist. If it were simply of an artist's model, and one did not know the name of the subject, the canvas would be a charming one. The almost childlike expression of ingenuous appeal, the great eyes and sensitive mouth, the modesty of expression, full of dignity nevertheless, as are also the virginal white robes, the whole attitude as if of surprise and deprecation at being thus painted as a personage, are in reality not the artist's dream, the fancy sketch of a type of feminine loveliness and sweetness, but the president of Wellesley College herself,—and every inch a president,—with intellectual powers trained to the utmost.

I doubt if any one can appreciate her pictures who fails to supplement them with that instantaneous illumination which came to her face the moment she spoke. It was a kind of inner light which I have never seen on any other face of man or woman.

When some girls had been talking foolishly, though apparently half aware that what they said was folly, she told them to stop, and added, "I'm glad I never was a girl."

She said, "Susan, you care too much about things; take them less seriously. The best of them won't run away."

She told me, "They hated me when I first came to Wellesley. I had charge of the work in the dining room and I made the girls attend to it. They had fallen into slack ways and resisted. But hate does n't last long in good girls."

One day I went to her in great indignation: "The doctor says I must go home, and I don't want to." "Very well," she said, "it is n't I who send you. So don't let us fall out about it. Sit down, talk it over, and let us see if we can plan to persuade the doctor to change his mind." As it gradually appeared that I must go and must be quiet for a time, she said, "It requires more courage to meet the daily tasks of a dull life than to rise for a moment to a great occasion. Don't you think it would be easier to submit to a surgical operation, and be done with it, than to sit still for a year and have some one stick pins into you?"

A certain senior of my class was habitually late at chapel. For a time this passed unnoticed. One morning, after everybody else was seated and the hymn was about to be given out, this senior opened the door. Miss Freeman fixed her eyes on her, followed her with them all the way down the aisle until she took her place in the middle of the front row. "*Now,*" said she, "we will sing the 164th hymn." The rebuke of her eyes and her emphasis were not to be forgotten. That was all she ever said about the matter, but it did not occur again.

One year many of us grew lazy and fell into the habit of sitting during the hymn. One morning Miss Freeman said quietly, but with her own look of humorous determination, "We will *rise* and sing the 23d hymn — 'Stand up, stand up for Jesus.'" Of course we rose, and kept on rising. Equally of course we were diverted by the cleverness which made any chiding word unnecessary.

Her self-control was instantaneous. As a little child, she had been frightened by seeing a cat in a fit, and she had ever after an instinctive aversion to cats. One morning at the chapel service, when she was leading the prayer with her eyes closed, a cat strayed upon the platform, jumped to her chair, and then to the desk upon her folded hands. Without the least quiver of voice to indicate that she had noticed anything, and without opening her eyes, she laid a hand upon the cat, pressed her gently down until the prayer was ended, then just before the last word quietly dropped her to the floor.

She raised the money for the building of a new dormitory, but there was great delay in finishing it. The contractors were late, the workmen dawdled. Finally she went to the director of the works and quietly said, "We move into this building on such a day." He answered, "Impossible. It will not be finished." "We shall be sorry to inconvenience your workmen, but we move on that day." The director stormed, made remarks about "ignorant women, unsexing themselves by trying to boss men." But wonders were accomplished, and on the day in question we moved in with comparatively little left to be done.

An Englishman came to the college one day. After inspecting it pretty fully and admiring its beauty, completeness, and cheerful effect on its students, he was still perplexed by its strangeness and by the readjustment of social conditions which it seemed to imply. "But, Miss Freeman," he inquired, "will not the four years here interfere with a girl's chances?" "Possibly they will," Miss Freeman answered, "her chances with men of a certain type. But I don't believe she will mind."

Walking with her once, I said, "Miss Freeman, there is a quality I long to possess more than any other, and that is tact. Probably it is inborn. Certainly it is very difficult to acquire. But you are the most tactful person I ever knew. Can't you give me some hint to help me a little toward tactfulness?" Unassumingly she disclaimed any such power. She wished she had it. She had tried to get it, and had been encouraged to do so by a former teacher. A teacher of her girlhood had told her about the importance of tact and had said that a good way to gain it was to care more about the person we are dealing with, and the end we seek, than about gaining that end by our special means. In working with others, he believed we often reach our end soonest if we are willing to set aside the way we know to be best and let others take the way they like best. So long as they are moving in our direction, and we are keeping close to them, he thought we ought to be satisfied.

My mother likes to recall the Sunday vesper service just before I graduated. Mother was a really great singer, with a reputation in England for oratorio solo work. She sang always, whenever she could give pleasure to anybody. The college kept her pretty busy during her week there. That Sunday night Miss Freeman sat far back in the chapel. As mother left the room, she came, like an impulsive child, and threw her arms around mother's neck and told her tearfully what the music had meant to her. I have always thought that her power lay partly in her presentation of the child in connection with the forceful woman.

My first glimpse of her was in my senior year. College did not begin till the morrow, and we were having a royal time over home boxes and summer news, when some one reported that we had a new professor of history, that she was to be our senior class officer, and that now was a propitious time to make her acquaintance and test her quality. A delegation waited on her and brought her, youthful as the youngest of us, bright, alert, charming — her fine, soft, brown hair combed back from her brow to a dainty coil behind, escaping in waves, making merry with itself here and there, her round, full face shining with delight to be counted one of us. She won us then and there, and forever.

I did not see her from that time, when she appeared in all her youthful beauty and freshness, until after the first year of her presidency. It was only three years as men count time, but many years had elapsed if we reckon what had been accomplished. A greater Wellesley had been evolved, and our lady showed marks of the effort. I looked at her twice before I, her warm and intimate companion of three years before, recognized her. Her hair was smoothly parted. She had donned some sort of lace arrangement; for at twenty-seven and as president of a college one needs external signs of age — though all this was soon abandoned. The evolution of the new Wellesley had drawn lines over the round, mobile face, lines of character, of strength, lines to be welcomed, for they stood for development and growth. She was changed and Wellesley was changed. She had reached out her hand and spanned the distance between Wellesley and Boston, between Wellesley and Cambridge. We were no longer sufficient to ourselves, shut away from the larger life at our doors, narrow, constrained, dogmatic, exclusive. At a bound our infancy was left behind. It is marvelous to look back upon the inspired intelligence with which she guided Wellesley through that rapid development.

Some of the loudest mourners over her departure from Wellesley were the little children of the neighborhood, for whom from time to time she used to hold "baby parties" on the college green. One little fellow of four uttered his lamentation so freshly that she cherished the remembrance of it. When his mother told him that Miss Freeman was going away from Wellesley, he broke into convulsive sobs; nor could he be quieted with assurances that she was not going far away, but would be very near, at Cambridge, where he might sometimes see her. "No, no, mama!" he cried, "You don't understand. It is n't the farness nor the nearness that I mind. It's the never-the-sameness."

Every place connected with her is filled with her joyous vitality. Here I see her writing letters, running down the hall; can catch her laugh, and her excite-

MONUMENT IN MEMORY OF MRS. PALMER

Designed by Daniel Chester French
Erected in Wellesley College Chapel by
Edwin Hale Abbot

ment over the interests of others. I recall how, when I went into a room where she was, she seemed the whole thing; and that when she went out, there was nothing left. As often as I think of her, I am ashamed of not being always hopeful and happy.

We loved her for the loving thoughts which sped
  Straight from her heart, until they found their goal
  In some perplexed or troubled human soul,
And broke anew the ever living bread.
We loved the mind courageous, which no dread
  Of failure ever daunted, whose control
  Of gentleness all opposition stole;
We loved herself and all the joy she shed.
O Leader of the Leaders! Like a light
  Thy life was set, to counsel, to befriend.
Thy quick and eager insight seized the right
  And shared the prize with bounteous hand and free.
  Fed from the fountains of infinity
Thy life was service, having love to spend.

PRESIDENT CAROLINE HAZARD.

IX

MARRIAGE

In his delightful "Theory of the Moral Sentiments" Adam Smith points out that each of us has certain emotions so entirely his own that to talk of them in public is improper. Suitable enough in themselves, they are not suitable for conversation. For the law of good manners is dictated by the possibility of sympathy. To express to another person feelings which are so little his that he cannot fully sympathize with them is to be rude to him and indecent as regards oneself. With this principle cultivated society is substantially in accord and sharply resents disclosures of private joys and sorrows. It is true we give license to poets and novelists, and praise them in proportion as they reveal the intimacies of the human heart. But it is the universal human heart, and not the special operations of John's or Susan's, which they reveal. Only as one's own experience is typical of that of others should it be made public.

That marriage is a matter more of private than of public concern is obvious; for while its larger emotions and circumstances are as generally apprehensible as other events of the day, these are tinged throughout with what Adam Smith calls "a peculiar turn of imagination," which is the lover's own and cannot be shared without a kind of impiety. I should naturally, therefore, pass Miss Freeman's marriage by with a bare record, if it did not present certain typical features and involve problems of general public concern. It excited much debate at the time, and probably influenced more people for good or ill than any other event of her life. Its hopes, courage, and sacrifices show the largeness of her womanhood. These aspects of it I must set forth. A biography which attempts to trace the inner growth of that beautiful character must give to this a central place.

Professor Horsford of Cambridge was an early friend of Mr. Durant's. He became chairman of the board of visitors of the college and one of its most frequent benefactors. Over Miss Freeman he watched with a father's tenderness. To his house she often came, and largely through him she became known in Cambridge. Her administration of Wellesley was much admired there. I had heard her praises sung for several years before I met her at Professor Horsford's house in 1884. In 1886, when I was publishing some papers on the elective system, I came to know her better, especially as in that year I gave a course of lectures at Wellesley. During the summer of 1886 Mrs. Governor Claflin and she visited Boxford, my country home. From that time our intimacy ripened rapidly until on her thirty-second birthday, February 21, 1887, I brought her an engagement ring. With characteristic audacity she insisted on wearing it at once. When at our next meeting I asked if her girls had not remarked it, she said they had on that very evening; but that when she had told them it was her birthday and this was one of her birthday gifts, she started a discussion over their respective ages and the subject of the ring disappeared. It did not disappear from her finger, however, necessary though concealment was. We both understood how badly the college and her work would be upset if our relations were talked of before the end of the term. I therefore stayed away from Wellesley, and nobody, not even the members of our two families, learned until summer that the new tie was formed. Immediately after Commencement Miss Freeman called a meeting of the Trustees and laid the whole matter before them.

My hope had been that she would be set free from Wellesley at once, and the wedding take place during the summer. In view of this she had already made some preliminary inquiries about a successor, inquiries which had little other result than to show how narrow was the range of choice. But the Trustees could not be brought to an immediate decision.

To lose Miss Freeman was in their view to imperil Wellesley, and naturally enough they wished for time to look about. They urged her to remain one year more, during which a successor might be sought, while both the public mind and the internal affairs of the college would become adjusted to the new order. From their point of view the plan was wise. Miss Freeman's devotion to duty, too, answered the appeal of their fears and made any defence of her own advantage distressing. I remember how we went driving on one of those perplexing days, and how as we passed farther into the solitary woods her spirits broke into girlish glee over the prospect of our home. She sang, laughed, jested, spoke low. Suddenly our road left the woods, and we found ourselves again on the shore of Lake Waban, with the college in full sight across the water. Her merriment stopped. Her face sobered and soon showed positive anguish. "How can I?" she said after a minute's silence. I could not bring the glad mood back. Sadly and with few more words we drove into the college grounds. Unhappily, at a time when this call of the college was especially strong, I gave way and agreed to let her remain in service until Christmas. It was barbarous to abandon her thus to the wolves. The damage done her health by those cruel months lasted for years; and in December Professor Helen A. Shafer was appointed her successor, — the same excellent person who had been designated in July. My futile repentance I here record.

But graver questions than that of date were involved in our marriage. Miss Freeman's youth and beauty ruling so skilfully the fairyland of Wellesley had often brought her the title of "The Princess," and Tennyson's poem of that name had become associated with her work. Now its problem, private fulfilment against public service, was brought widely into debate. There were heated partisans on each side. On the one hand it was strongly argued that in proportion as one develops capacity for public things he should treat his personal desires as matters of little moment. Others should treat them so too. Priests cannot marry, and kings only those who are likely to promote the interests of their land. When a headstrong king resigns his crown to marry a beggar maid, it makes a pretty story, but a justly exasperated people. It is not tyranny to regulate the marriage of soldiers and sailors. Possibly artists should remain single. Responsibility carries with it trusts which cannot be cast away at will. Civilization rests upon dedicated lives, lives which acknowledge obligation not to themselves or to other single persons, but to the community, to science, to art, to a cause. Especially base was it for one who had proved her power to win an unwilling public to look with favor on the education of women now to snatch at the selfish seclusion of home, and so confirm the popular fancy that a woman will drop the weightiest charge if enticed with a bit of sentiment. What too must be thought of the man who would tempt her from eminence to obscurity?

Such distrustful remarks hurt Miss Freeman cruelly, and she was correspondingly grateful for the many kind words and letters which brought approval of her step. The Trustees and professors were especially generous. They understood her and now, with but one or two exceptions, rejoiced in her gain, regardless of their own loss. Yet to some even of them, as to many of the public, it was not at once evident why marriage should break her career and leave mine intact. Why should not I give way rather than she? Harvard is at no great distance from Wellesley. I had found my way across for injury; why not now for benefit? Many Harvard instructors live in neighboring towns. One might go to and fro each day from Wellesley. Or, better still, why not resign at Harvard and join her in the presidency? Then home and occupation would alike express our union. A friend of Wellesley offered to build us a house within the grounds there, and to raise a fund for the joint salary, though this was hardly necessary; her salary being at the time $4000 and mine but $3500, we should have been in easier circumstances at Wellesley than in Cambridge.

I have stated these adverse criticisms somewhat in detail because they all seem to me important. With most of them I am in hearty sympathy; indeed I was so even then, as appears in a letter recently sent me from Mrs. Claflin's papers and printed at the close of this chapter. But though in that letter some considerations are given which might well lessen Wellesley's sense of loss, I think I had better state here more systematically the reasons which at the time we thought set us free to act as love prompted. Our problem having been recognized as a somewhat general one, the grounds of our decision may properly have some general interest.

In the view of both of us Miss Freeman's work at Wellesley was already substantially done. In another six years she could accomplish little more than any creditable successor. She had set the pattern, and quiet growth according to it was what was now required. Little further constructive work was at the moment possible. From the dying hands of the founder she had received the rough outlines of a college. With consummate skill and originality she had set these in order, and filled them with such ideals as would insure their ultimate strength. But she was confined to a pioneer epoch, and its very conditions cut her off from sharing in the anticipated results. No college can be created at a word; it is a thing of growth. Especially is it true of a college started by a single founder that after its first active years there comes a considerable period of quiescence. Until the personal stamp has worn away, the public rightly will not adopt it. The Trustees selected by the founder must die, his Faculty be replaced, the resources of his fortune prove evidently insufficient, his private methods of administration go through a searching criticism, and he himself sink into a hazy and mythical figure, before the community will regard his college as really its own and a new group of givers be gathered for its support. All this requires time. It seemed to Miss Freeman and myself that having faithfully carried the college through its pioneer period, she might be discharged from its waiting time; that the length of this might even be diminished and the coming of a period of expansion be hastened by the withdrawal of one so closely associated with its founder. Much of the aid she could now give might be given as well in private life as from the president's chair. Of course she remained on the Board of Trustees, and was a close friend of the succeeding presidents.

But it might well be urged that even during the waiting years, though further enlargement was impossible, her ennobling presence could ill be spared. I thought, however, that so subordinate a benefit to the college should properly give way to the demands of her health. It will be remembered that she broke down during her first year at Wellesley. While she learned much from that experience, she had never been able to adopt the more indulgent modes of life which she knew to be necessary for full recovery. Her office claimed all her time and much more than her strength, allowing her only a single vacation in six years. The duties of a president are under the best conditions enormous, and present themselves with little regard to the needs of him who executes them. They crushed her two successors more quickly than herself. To-day we have learned better means of protection than were known then. President Hazard justly writes, "Twenty years ago there were fewer devices for labor-saving. Stenographers were not yet in the field, secretaries still wrote long-hand. So with scanty help, working day and night, living in the building with her girls, having them constantly in close association with her, giving unsparingly of herself, Miss Freeman lived her life." I did not think it safe that such exhaustion should continue. It was better even for the college that she should help it henceforth in other ways.

Obviously too these conditions cut me off from joining her at Wellesley; for while, if I were there, I could undoubtedly relieve her of much, I could not break up those habits of whole-hearted devotion which were at once her glory and her danger. But of course I had no idea of closing her career. Those who protested against this were quite right. Talents so obviously meant for mankind no one had a right to seize for himself. "Not mine, I never called her mine." Only on condition that I could give her enlargement, not confinement, was I justified in accepting her sacrifice and bearing her away to my home. Yet I thought our critics a little dull not to perceive the vast increase of powers which love, home, ease, and happiness bring. Until these fundamental needs are supplied, everybody in my judgment is only half himself. It is absurd then to look on these with suspicion and exalt a public career in contrast, when these are the very means by which that becomes rich and strong. The public person is not one being and the private another; for the worth of public leadership is pretty exactly proportioned to the wealth of the personal nature. So it had hitherto been in her case. To carry that wealth still nearer to completeness was my happy office. President Eliot's words are weighty: —

"After six years of masterly work at Wellesley College, in which she exhibited the keenest intelligence, large executive ability, and a remarkable capacity for winning affection and respect, she laid down these functions, married at the age of thirty-two, and apparently entered on a wholly new career. Alice Freeman thus gave the most striking testimony she could give of her faith in the fundamental social principle that love between man and woman, and the family life which results therefrom, afford for each sex the conditions of its greatest usefulness and honor, and of its supreme happiness. The opponents of the higher education of women had always argued that such education would tend to prevent marriage and to dispossess the family as the cornerstone of society. Alice Freeman gave the whole force of her conspicuous example to disprove that objection. She illustrated in her own case the supremacy of love and of family life in the heart of both man and woman."

I have said that I weakly agreed to have Miss Freeman remain at Wellesley until December. Each Sunday of those autumn months I spent with her there, becoming more fully acquainted with the college and the life which she was soon to lay down. In these last months she was doubly anxious to do her utmost for her beloved college, and everybody who had any subject on which she might be consulted with advantage took this opportunity to see her. Girls and colleagues hastened to get one final draught of inspiration. Love is merciless, and often crowds so close to its adored object as almost to trample it down. Then too the conflicting claims of home and college tore her night and day. A severer period of toil she never experienced. Fortunately a limit was fixed by the Harvard Christmas recess, extending from December 23 to January 3. The first of these days, falling in 1887 on Friday, was set for the wedding. She had decided to be married at the house of Governor and Mrs. Claflin, 65 Mt. Vernon Street, Boston, which had been one of her dearest places of refuge since she first came to Wellesley. Her parents' home was too far away. As I was living in chambers, Cambridge was out of the question; and she could not get rid of a feeling that to be married in the Wellesley Chapel would give her personal affairs excessive prominence. The wedding was at half-past eleven in the morning. Up to that hour of the previous night she worked in her college office.

LETTERS

BOXFORD, July 8, 1887.

DEAR MRS. CLAFLIN:

I hear from Miss Freeman that she has told you of our engagement. I am very glad she has. You would naturally be one of the first whom we should wish to tell. You have known us as few others among the Trustees have, and in the excited discussions that are to come there will be plenty of need of clear knowledge, in order to make people turn away from their hot momentary feeling and consider the real facts in the case. This great service of keeping people just and clear-headed you can now do for Miss Freeman. She will need such protection. She is greatly strained already. You know how sensitive she is to the disapproval of those she loves, even when she sees that their disapproval springs from nothing better than half knowledge. To hint that she is abandoning duty for selfish gains is to cut her with a knife. We all perceive that she is incapable of doing such a thing, but her pain is just as great as if she were.

On the other hand, that people will abuse me I anticipate, and I think it very proper that they should. Being of tolerably tough material, I can stand abuse very comfortably. In the place of a Wellesley Trustee, I dare say I should denounce this thievish Harvard professor pretty roundly. And yet I hold that at the present moment I am one of the great benefactors of Wellesley, one of the few who clearly see the direction in which its prosperity lies. Let me explain the paradox.

Great causes and great institutions are generally best founded, or guided through crises, by a single leader. They are embodiments of him. His is their inspiration and his their wisdom. The service of them is personal allegiance. To him everything is referred, and his will takes for the time the place of all more minute law and organization. Wellesley has fortunately had this experience, first under Mr. Durant and then under the general of his choice. But the danger which besets such an institution is obvious: it does not acquire a life of its own. Everything is staked on the single leader; and even when that leader is perfect, there is something lacking in the spontaneous vigor of the separate parts. It is beautiful to see how the greatest of all leaders perceived this and said to his disciples, "It is expedient for you that I go away, although because I go sorrow hath filled your hearts." He knew that fulness of life could come about only in that way.

Now you know that ever since I have been acquainted with you, and before I loved Miss Freeman, I pointed out that this must be the next stage in Wellesley's growth. I held that it was now about ready for it. There is always something green and immature in an institution that hangs much on a single person. It is in unstable equilibrium. Solid organizations welcome great men, but are not dependent on them. A Western college may die if it does not get a suitable president; the great universities of Germany change their rectors every two years, and are totally unaffected.

You and I believe in Miss Freeman's work. We think it has been strong and far-seeing. We hold that she has set the college on the right paths and has not only done herself, but has shown others how to do. If this is our belief, we have nothing to be afraid of in the present change. The time of testing her work is come, and we can be calm, sure that whatever the temporary hardship, here is an opportunity for the college to take a great step forward.

You will readily suppose that in my mind these are no new thoughts. For Wellesley I am something like the enthusiast that you are, and this ennobling friendship of mine with Miss Freeman could not deepen from year to year and month to month without often calling me to consider what right I had to such a share in her. The advantage I have must be the advantage of the public too. Unless I had believed it might be so, I would have turned away. I do believe it; and as I come nearer, I believe it more and more. I now know — what I did not at first — that those who clamor for her remaining longer at Wellesley, while believing themselves public-spirited are doing a cruelly selfish thing. They are asking her to give what she has already spent, and spent too for their sakes. If they really love her and are grateful for her work, they will beg her to leave. My chief fear is that it is already too late. If I had never appeared, she could not go on two years longer. But my hope is that by constant watchfulness and by the warm strength of a home — which to her, since she is a human being, is no less precious than it is to those who will blame her — I may do something to restore powers already seriously shaken and may succeed in making of her a great buttress, a strong outside support, for Wellesley through many years.

It is pleasant to think too that my own opportunities for helping Wellesley will now be much increased.

But these things are not the main object of my letter. I am really writing an invitation. I want you to visit me here a week from Saturday, and to bring Miss Freeman with you. Here we will have more of those restful days which grow only in these pleasant fields. The past months have brought some hardships, among them these: that for the sake of the college I thought I had no right to visit Wellesley — which I saw but once between March and Commencement — and then that for the same reason I have been forced into silence with my friends. Now there is a glad relief from restraint. Alice and I have been perfectly free in expressing to you our interest in one another while we were only friends; and now that our friendship has gone through and through us, we want you with us still; for you know as few others can how exceptional is our union — occupations and tastes and principles and experience already harmonized before we marry, and our powers sufficiently unlike to give us the wealth of diversity. I am sure that you who are not afraid of sentiment will, if with some momentary regrets, still give us your hearty approval and, as I hope, your presence here.

With warm regard, I am,

Sincerely yours,

G. H. Palmer.

You ought not to be abroad this bright summer Sunday, but here where we could talk to our heart's content of many, many things. Your good letter made me sorry that you have met disappointments everywhere in your wanderings, but I hope you have found the clear air invigorating for your sister. Then I am sure you will be contented. I shall not go abroad this summer. I need the rest badly, and ought to go and take it immediately. But perhaps I can do better. It is of this that I want to write you to-day. So go away by yourself before you read my next page. It is cruel that I cannot be near to comfort you as I talk, because I think you will be very sorry, possibly angry; but sometime you will know that I am doing the best thing I can possibly do. For I am going to marry — sometime — and to marry Professor Palmer. Yes, dear, I know you think I ought not to leave the college, and are terribly grieved. You asked me once about him, but then we were not engaged. As soon as I can, I tell you; and I believe you will really be glad to have me take a quieter, longer life than I could otherwise have, a happier and a wiser one. Remember this when you come home and do not refuse to know my professor, but learn to love him for his own true sake — not merely for mine. And won't you read German with me this year? I must revive my languages as fully as possible, for I suppose the following summer we go abroad.

I am just dressed, dear father, for the first time since Monday; and now it is Thursday afternoon. An intermittent fever has got hold of me and a bad cough, especially nights and mornings. I had no appetite, and the constant feeling of weakness wore me out and sent me to bed last Monday. Now I am better, and I want to talk about plans for the summer instead of about myself all the time. My engagement is announced, and I have promised the Trustees to remain as president for a part of next year. So you will be pleased, quite satisfied I hope. I make up a bundle of these nice letters which have come from all over the country and share them with you. H. writes, "Ah, if we might have Professor Palmer here at Wellesley!" That is what so many are saying — all except the Harvard and Cambridge people — urging him to come to the college with me.

I wonder where you would like me to be married when the time comes. All his friends and the college people will wish the wedding here, for few could go so far as Michigan. But I would never consent to be married at the college unless every member of my family could be present, and I am not sure that I should like it even then. I can see that I shall be urged to let Wellesley have the pleasure of the wedding. Mr. Palmer would like to have it in the pleasant autumn weather, when it is so much easier to begin housekeeping than in the winter. Could you come East by that time? Yet our house in Saginaw is so pretty I should really like to have the wedding there, where it would be less conspicuous. A few people would like to come from here. Tell me what you think.

I snatch this little minute on the train going to Boston in order to get a word with you, my child. Can you read what I would say? On Friday morning, December 23, I am to be married in Boston, just Mr. Palmer's family and my own present. A few of our dearest friends are to be invited to meet us immediately afterwards. I wish my little girl could be there and meet her new father. But I will answer now the questions you have in mind. I am to be married in a long white *moire* dress, with point lace and veil, — to be a real bride, you see, — and my reception dresses are dark red velvet, white lace, white silk, and yellow satin. We go to housekeeping immediately in Cambridge.

It is now settled that we sail the first of July, and remain fifteen months abroad. I am sure the decision is wise, but I have many regrets, I love some people and colleges in and about Boston so much that this long absence is not coveted. Yet we both need to seize the opportunity at once. If we wait a year, with so many frail relatives on each side, we may not be able to go at all. We can go now, leaving all our friends in fair comfort and health; and a year hence return from rest and study a good deal better fitted for daily work. So I am making my farewell visit at home, leaving my husband to cope with a new cook alone. Why will good servants get married?

1888, December 23, 11.30 A. M. Dear Mrs. Claflin: You are the one who must share this hour. Do you know that *just* a year ago my George was taking me down the stairs into your beautiful rooms to make me a wife? So I must come back and end the perfect year as I began it, under the light of your smile. No one of us knew then how blessed a year was opening before two people. I wish I might sit down in your own room now and show you the symbol which has just been put on my hand. It is a great shining opal, set round with diamonds. When G. and I were in Paris four months ago we were strolling one night, looking into the jeweller's fascinating windows, and discovered an opal ring with tints of green and gold, richer and deeper than we had ever seen before. We looked at it with delight and often afterwards searched for it, but could never find it again. Fancy how my breath was taken away when just now that identical ring was put on my finger! That base deceiver had helped me look for it many a time after it was safely hidden in his pocket. And now here it is, with the splendor of the sun at its heart and changing into fresh beauty whenever I look at it. That, dear friend, is like married life, is n't it? All things made new every morning and evening. And it is good to have you so tied in with our greatest days. I think of you in connection with Boxford's sweet peace, with Wellesley's eager life, with all our married joy and work together. Let us see each other very often when I come home.

X

SABBATICAL YEARS

THREE out of the four divisions into which Mrs. Palmer's life naturally falls have now been described. First there was the period of Family Life, before she had acquired a life of her own; then that of Culture, when from early girlhood to university graduation she was busy with her own development; thirdly, that of Service, when the daily demands of other people dictated every act. Now with her marriage begins a period of Self-Expression, when she came to the full use of all her powers and in their joyous outgo so combined service and culture that it was impossible to say whether she labored for the benefit of others or for the mere fun of the thing. The latter was her own view. As she woke in the morning she would often say, "Here's another great rich day!" The glowing world was before her, and with it she was in complete accord. I have seen a puzzled look come over her face when her self-denial was praised. That was not the side from which she approached her duties; interest in them was her prompter. I sometimes think she was hardly more unselfish than others; only her selfishness excluded none of the affairs of those about her, but found its material there. From her earliest childhood there was stored in this exuberant and sympathetic nature provision for the union of aims which often conflict. It grew through all her bleak years, but reached its most exquisite and abundant fruitage only after she found herself in a sheltered home. There, though she still did the work of several men, bits of quiet could be interposed, her health was guarded and grew firm, the large range and variety of her influence prevented monotonous fatigue, and the happiness of her own dancing heart went forth to gladden all she did. Through strenuous seasons she had already gained

> The reason firm, the temperate will,
> Endurance, foresight, strength, and skill.

She now went on her joyous way exulting in their exercise.

During the spring of 1888 we occupied a furnished house in Cambridge, where Mrs. Palmer was warmly welcomed. Study was thrown to the winds; we devoted ourselves to resting, to becoming better acquainted with each other and with our neighbors. In a university town every newcomer must eat his way in, and during the course of his adoption as a member of the household attend a kindly series of dinners and teas. This process of making acquaintance was in our case begun by a luncheon in Mrs.

Palmer's honor given by President and Mrs. Eliot, and attended solely by the Harvard Faculty and their wives. Similar festivities filled our evenings. Our afternoons were occupied with calls; I remember making three hundred and forty in the course of the season. Mondays, the weekly holidays of Wellesley, we opened our door to Mrs. Palmer's former associates. Making a business of society was so novel to me that I was interested in watching its different effects on Mrs. Palmer and myself. For a time it puzzled me to know why at the end of a day of it she came out fresh and I exhausted. But I soon discovered that she had all the time been enjoying people, while I had been trying to enjoy them. For her, people always seemed necessary to enable her to breathe easily, their manifold interests to be her daily food. As she gradually adjusted herself to my studious ways, and I to her social ones, there came a double gain.

But her obvious need after so many years of labor was entire rest and change of scene. If so vital a creature could be rendered torpid for a time, she would be sure to come forth with heightened powers. For just such periodic renewal there exists a happy provision at Harvard, this being the first university to establish the Sabbatical Year. Each seventh year, it is arranged, a professor may take to himself on half pay. He need not teach or study, he may travel or remain at home, he may even altogether decline the proffered vacation and go on with customary work and salary; but the opportunity is given to freshen and enrich himself, and by doing so to enrich his subsequent teaching. Only five years before, I had enjoyed such a vacation, but the authorities of the University, perceiving Mrs. Palmer's need, offered me another prematurely. I accepted it; we went abroad in June, remaining away for more than a year. Three such Sabbatical Years we had, in 1888, 1895, and 1902, important periods in Mrs. Palmer's life, yet interruptions of its current. Being detachable from the rest of her story, I will treat them all here indiscriminately, in connection with the first. Nor will I set down their incidents chronologically, but rather indicate the general methods of recuperation pursued in them and thus attempt to exhibit in its lighter moments a character which has hitherto appeared too sedate.

Mrs. Palmer was an excellent loafer. I had some misgivings on this point at first, remembering how perniciously habituated she was to industry. In going abroad I felt that my chief object must be to teach her to eat, sleep, and loaf. But she required no teaching, and took to all these useful arts instinctively. In fact they had been the secret of her past endurance. She never worried. When a job was completed, or not yet ready to attack, she turned her mind to other things. During her severest times at Wellesley she slept soundly and immediately. Once in later life, after a public address, when she was about to take a train for another engagement, a worn woman pressed forward with the question, "Mrs. Palmer, how are you able to do so much more than other persons?" The time only permitted a witty epigram, but she packed it with truth. "Because," she answered, "I have n't any nerves nor any conscience, and my husband says I have n't any backbone." A prosaic letter came the next day inquiring whether one could altogether dispense with a conscience. She could, when work was over. Into a holiday no schoolgirl of twelve ever carried a lighter heart. Her very aptitudes for business fitted her also for recreation, since whatever was appropriate to the moment, even idleness, got at once her full attention. Such intentional methods of escaping responsibility were greatly assisted too by the native nimbleness of her physical senses, her response to natural beauty, the vivacious interest she took in every moving thing, and her disposition to fill small matters with romance.

The aim then of our Sabbatical Years not being intellectual or social profit, we sought seclusion and avoided sight-seeing. Seldom did we go out of an evening, and we carried no letters of introduction. Europe we took as our playground. We should have remained at home if anywhere in America we could have escaped business and people; but against these attractive enemies of the worn-out man there is no barrier like the ocean. We accordingly moved about as little as possible; and if we ever went to popular resorts, we went there out of season. We did not visit Norway or Russia, Asia, Africa, or Spain — all these parts requiring a large amount of travel. Our taste turned to places where greater enjoyment could be had with smaller fatigue. Rome, too, we generally avoided, as the place where all the world is engaged in afternoon tea. Our chief demand was domestic comfort, with a minor welcome for pleasing scenes or handy galleries and libraries. Sunshine we also desired, but learned how rarely it can be had in a European winter. That the sun works throughout the year is apparently a discovery of Columbus, our America showing between its wintry storms such skies as Europe seldom sees. One spends weeks abroad without the sun. For half the year the gray day is in fashion; while the feeling of the American is that it is the business of clouds to rain, and that when not engaged in this they should leave the sky. But finding that pretty much the same gloom obtained everywhere, we thought we profited most by long stays in single places. When after a few months the sense of repose began to wear down into incipient monotony, we would interpose a few weeks of brisk travel before settling again in some spot widely different from the previous home. To the making of these successive homes we thought a few familiar objects useful. Usually we carried about with us a tablecloth, clock, hearth-rug, and many books. The distribution of these made even hotel rooms homelike.

But hotels were little to our liking, especially those designed for foreigners. Finding that in *pensions* we had still less privacy, we usually took furnished rooms, hired a maid, and set up housekeeping. In Germany, for any brief period, this is impossible, the ubiquitous government invading the kitchen and prescribing the length and conditions of service. But in France and Italy most comfortable apartments can be had at rates far below those of the large hotels. Ours usually had three chambers, with parlor, dining room, and kitchen. Of the many servants who have been with us in all parts of Europe we never found one incompetent or dishonest, a record almost incredible to our oppressed housekeepers. To several we became warmly attached. In America servants are usually helots — a subject people of alien nationality. In Europe they differ little from other persons except in the matter of means. We found several of great intelligence and dignity, but perhaps I ought to add that we never employed those who spoke English. They do not keep their quality after mixing much with foreigners. We generally obtained them through the *concierge*, and to them entrusted most of our marketing. It was always honestly done, at least it was done for less than I could do it. No doubt in order to select a good servant or *concierge* one should be a fair judge of human nature; but he who is not will hardly find ease in any relation of life.

On coming to a city we ordinarily went to a small hotel. From this I sallied forth to explore the streets which struck me as best adapted for residence. Cards in the windows show whether there are apartments to let and if they are furnished. I seldom inquired the price, but mentioned what I was prepared to pay. Nor did I ever engage on a first visit; but after looking into ten or twenty houses, I made a list of the three or four that pleased me and reported them to Mrs. Palmer. These we then inspected together, comparing their unlike advantages, and usually were soon able to reach a satisfactory decision. But we did not feel compelled to accept what was merely pretty good, our faith being that in every city there were just the cheerful rooms we wished, and at our own price, if we could only find them; and never were we disappointed in our pleasant game of hide and seek. A little pains spent in the search saves much disappointment in the residence. Some American fears, too, proved groundless: difficulties did not arise in drawing the contract at hiring, nor on leaving were we charged with improper damages. That such things occur I do not doubt, but certainly they cannot be common. Of course out of season one has his best choice of rooms, gets them on his own terms, and keeps them only so long as he pleases. We have sometimes set up a home for a single month. The total expense of such an establishment — lodging, food, servant, washing, fees, and flowers, this last an important item — never exceeded thirty francs a day for the two. Often it was much less.

Such a home once discovered is available afterwards. The happiness formerly enjoyed in it is preserved and greets him who returns. There are familiar faces and street-cries. The chair has a better place by the fire than in other rooms, and the bed yields sounder sleep. One is obliged to form no new habits, and the means of access to the pleasant places of the town are understood without inquiry. So we soon acquired favorite haunts. Grasmere, among the English Lakes, was one of them, where we lived with Wordsworth, the wild roses, the rattling ghylls, and the mists which curl about the slaty peaks. To these gracious scenes we usually turned on landing from the ocean, and would end the London shopping in time to spend among them the week before sailing home. Paris and Venice and Florence and the University of my boyhood, Tübingen in Germany, always claimed us. Each of these is a city of the soul and completely sums up a single mental attitude.

In Paris can be had more exactly the kind of life one wishes, whatever that kind may be, than perhaps in any other city on earth. All is clean and tasteful, well regulated, but without the intrusions of Germany. The French, it is true, are the Chinese of Europe, and possess an intelligence rigidly circumscribed by custom and locality. They lean helplessly on institutions, have small individual power, and little curiosity about anything which does not fall within their usual experience. Deep insights, resulting in beauty, invention, or religion, are therefore denied them. But prettiness abounds, convenience, dignified courtesies and ceremonials. The people are kind and attachable. Such matters are worth more to visitors than the profounder constituents of life. Indeed they impart better the desired sense of foreignness, the very restrictions of the French mind, — its inability to move beyond the limits of its language, land or etiquette, — quickly forcing the stranger to feel that he is far from that country of his own which he would for the moment forget.

Sometimes we were in new Paris, on the Rue Galilée, just off the Champs Élysées — that matchless avenue which more than any other city street thrills the beholder and invites him to loiter or to sit. There too the Bois was at hand and flight to the country easy. Sometimes we lived in the Latin Quarter — more Latin then than now — haunting Notre

Dame, the bookshops on the Quays, the lectures at the Sorbonne, the admirable plays and *conférences* of the Odéon, the student restaurants. Really to know Mrs. Palmer one should see her as a merry girl in a French *pâtisserie* or on an omnibus top. We usually spent the morning at home, had an early *déjeuner* and then for exercise went into the country, walked the Long Gallery of the Louvre, — where one may not sit, — looked into some church, took a seat in a steamboat on the river, or hunted up some spot connected with the Commune or the greater Revolution. Enlarging one's acquaintance with a foreign language is a happy way of wasting a large amount of time; and this makes it one of the fittest sabbatical occupations for a busy pair. Mrs. Palmer, however, would occasionally turn aside from paths of rectitude and visit schools.

This description of our modes of life in Paris applies, *mutatis mutandis*, to Venice and Florence, only that Venice was the one spot in Europe which best met Mrs. Palmer's ideas of Paradise. She loved it with romantic passion, walking its winding alleys, inhabiting its churches, and sitting in its Piazza and Academy as if all belonged to her. The Venetians have fashioned their own world. Into it they have admitted abundantly religion, law, and sensuous enjoyment, and thought of these always as friendly. Everywhere they have demanded beauty, and taken the kind they preferred rather than the inherited types. All this was congenial to her. Loving pictures as she did, she prized every gallery in proportion to the number of its Venetian masters. In the beautiful city itself she cared as much for the works of nature as for those of man, for in it the two ever intermingle. Its morning and evening lights she thought lovelier than elsewhere, as was also the foliage which at intervals overhangs the watery streets, or the sky sharply cut by the graceful architecture. We spent an entire winter there, besides making shorter stays at every possible season, living generally in an old palace on the Grand Canal, a little beyond Sta. Maria della Salute.

To each, however, of the years we passed abroad we took care to assign some novel feature. This kept the sameness refreshing. One Spring we spent in Greece, going to Ithaca, to Delphi, and Olympia. Greek had early been a favorite study of Mrs. Palmer's, and she came to the enjoyment of that unique sculpture and architecture not unprepared. It is impossible to knock the beauty out of a piece of marble which a Greek hand has touched. While a fragment remains, the master is there. She at least found no difficulty in overlooking absent heads and legs, and easily turned her mind to the loveliness that is left. Greek gravestones she learned to know in Athens for the first time, and was deeply moved by their method of proclaiming no grief, but resting in some remembered scene from the life of him who had gone. She gathered all procurable photographs of them, as of the splendid tombs of Italy, and placed them together in a book which she called her Graveyard. Yet she enjoyed Greece not merely because the Greeks had enjoyed it, but for the same reasons as they. Its colored soils, the noble outlines of its heights, its atmosphere, its ever present sea, its olive trees, intoxicated her and kept her from regretting its generally absent verdure. She interested herself too in its present conditions and people. Dr. Schliemann was hospitable. The accomplished sister of Prime Minister Tricoupis became her friend.

But our greatest novelty, and the one to which her thoughts afterwards most often recurred, was our bicycling — a sport now almost exterminated by the exciting and lazy automobile. One year we carried our wheels from America and, starting from Rouen, rode through Normandy, Brittany, and parts of Picardy and Provence; then over the Corniche Road from Fréjus to Alassio; we crossed the three hundred and sixty miles of Styria and Carinthia lying between Venice and Vienna; rode through the Black Forest from Tübingen to Freiburg; and at the close took some stretches of central England. Altogether our cyclometers registered over fifteen hundred miles. When we left home she had sat on a bicycle only three times; but as she had the queer characteristic of doing excellently and at once whatever she did, on our first day in Normandy she rode eighteen miles with entire ease.

The sport of bicycling suited Mrs. Palmer's passion for independence as did little else. Ready as her sympathies regularly were, she was no less ready, when the burden of the world became oppressive, to throw them all aside. Then she would renew herself in utter freedom and isolation, afterwards coming forth ardently social again. In her the child and the responsible woman were ever amusingly combined. It was the former that steered when she sat on her bicycle. At the call of the white road she felt all ties to be cut. The world was all before her where to choose. She could turn to the right or left, could feel the down-pressed pedal and the rushing air, could lie in the shade by the roadside, visit a castle, dally long at luncheon, gather grapes or blackberries from the field, stop at whatever small inn might attract at night, and for days together commune rather with nature than with man. To preserve the fullest sense of independence we sent forward no trunk to meet us at appointed spots, but designed a soft bag for the bicycle which would hold supplies for three weeks. We made our nights long, beginning to ride about half-past nine in the morning and ending in time for the bath and rest before dinner. We rode slowly, avoiding records of more than forty miles a day, and dismounting at every colorable excuse; our rule for hills being that wherever a horse should walk, we would. Nor did we practise anything like continuous riding. A week or two on the bicycle was generally put in between two periods of housekeeping; though if we happened in one of our jaunts on any specially charming village, we lingered as long as the charm continued. Of course we kept clear of railroads and tourist regions, and so were able to meet the common people in their homes and fields. Among the peasants we learned always to make our inquiries of the women, who are far less lumpish than the men. They take the produce to market, supervise the children, and in general manage the intellectual side of the farm. In consequence they have their wits about them and are often capable of an immediate answer. To bring the man's mind into action requires at least three questions.

Such were our vacation years. From them what stores of health and courage were borne away! What vivid pictures were stored in memory, subsequently to be the joy, not of solitude, but of crowded and parted days! What happy intimacy of companionship was had when two, always close in heart, but ordinarily much separated by occupation, could for a long period honorably make each other their sole concern!

LETTERS

Tell us of Cambridge and Wellesley. We are hungry for every scrap of news of them, in spite of the bliss in which we find ourselves here. And really in our part of Lucerne all is like the story-book happenings. Our big sunny room has east and south windows, and our poetical balcony, furnished with tables and chairs, overhangs a charming garden, laid out with rare trees and shrubs along its winding walks, and sloping to the bright green waters of the lake. All day below us gay little boats and busy steamers hurry by, or float as lazily as the hundreds of swans and ducks among them. And always the mountains guard us. Before us is the Titlis glacier; to the right and left Pilatus and the Rhighi. Here we sojourn for a happy fortnight.

We have been on the Continent nearly a month; and our few days in England were delightful, in spite of the rain. The fragrance of our drives and walks in the English Lake country, our talks and readings there, will follow me to gray hairs. London itself was then as now suffering a deluge. We sought refuge in the British Museum and National Gallery. In such arks one could pass a forty days' flood comfortably, but we deserted them as soon as our watertight boots were made, and floated over to Rotterdam. You know how we two are always lighting on good fortune. On that passage we had the only stateroom of the boat. This gave us an easy night, with unspeakable miseries all around. Do you grow callous every day in Europe to the woes of humanity? Or do you stay awake nights with your unhappy fellow-mortals, as helpless as they?

Our chief resting place between London and here was Tübingen, where G. once spent two years at the University. I wanted to know the quaint town. So we settled for ten days at the Golden Lamb, with our windows looking out on the Markt Platz, where peasant women sat all day beside their fruit and vegetable baskets. Each night the storks came home from the fields, and with their long legs perching on the housetops looked solemnly down on their neighbors' red peaked roofs, in proper fairy story fashion. There I had my first experience of German dinner parties; for the professors were most hospitable and gave us extraordinary entertainments. Such mysterious pyramids of unknown contents, into which I unblushingly plunged as the guest of honor, trembling inwardly, and without a notion of how they should be attacked. Ought one to make the onset on the east or west tower, or strike directly at the base? Then the wild efforts to discuss American and German affairs with their English and my South German! Well, that week in the Fatherland was memorable; and in spite of the novelty of formal toasts at the dinners, they were good dinners and the people endlessly kind and thoughtful. In Suabia even the conductors and old women treated me as if I were a long lost grandchild.

This fragrant green sunny valley is so fair to look upon! The peasant girls are raking the thick hay on steep slopes; old women are drying their clothes in the spicy air; cattle and goats are climbing among the rocks for the juicy grass, and the sound of their many bells and the cries of the herdsmen and shepherds come like music from afar; and always night and day the Fiescher-Bach rushes and tumbles by our windows on its way from the glacier just around the shoulder of the mountain to join the river below. It seems as if the brooks and bells were in another world and we heard them in dreams only.

We have mounted up to this height through successive steps. First came the valleys, with cottages and fields; then rich green slopes; a little higher, forests of pine and fir; above these, the red-brown heather with broken granite rocks, sometimes scattered here and there, sometimes piled in high masses; and still above, desolations which look as if a world had been shattered in pieces and heaped against the sky. Making our way among millions of boulders of granite, slate, and marble, we find patches of snow, and finally we reach the snow fields themselves and look out upon the most extensive system of glaciers which Europe can show, — four in sight at once, — the largest fifteen miles long. It looks like a wide frozen river, the surface seamed and scarred, winding its way fearfully among the craggy peaks.

On reaching Paris we went to the little native hotel which L. mentioned and found it as pleasant as he promised, except that we could get no sunshine there. So G. set forth to find "the sunniest pleasantest rooms in Paris at a merely nominal rent." I laughed when he came home the first night, his pedometer showing that he had walked twelve miles. The second day he walked fourteen. But he had found an apartment which we took for two months the instant I saw it. I should be relieved if I could have rooms so beautiful in Cambridge. They cover an entire fourth floor — third, they call it here. You should see our pretty parlor. It, and every room as well, has an open fire-place. We burn soft coal and wood, and always have the cheer of a blaze on our hearth. The carpet is dark red and brown. At the three long windows are white lace curtains with red hangings. We have two red sofas, three arm-chairs, and five others all covered with the same plush. The centre table has our cover on it, with a bowl of dahlias in the middle. At the side of the room is a rosewood writing desk, with convenient drawers; and near the fire-place a little bookcase with our books, a blossoming plant on its top. Three good pictures are on the walls, which are themselves decorated tastefully with panels, carvings, and mirrors. The dining room and three chambers are no less charming.

Our servant can neither speak nor understand a word of anything except French, but she is a creature of so many perfections that I hesitate to catalogue them. With Marie Louise in charge, French housekeeping is play. We are growing fat under her providing care. She does our marketing and restricts all extravagance. But she puts such an exquisite flavor into her dishes as makes us grieve over her small outlay. We have protested against *two* as a limit to pieces of bread, chops, etc. I think she eats nothing herself. We have been compelled to forbid her cleaning the whole apartment every day, for we were sometimes kept up at night by her labors with the dust-cloth. She feels the deprivation, and when we announce that we are going out to Marly or Fontainebleau, she indulges in a genuine spring cleaning. After doing everything else, she searches my clothes to find a possible stitch to take, and takes it most daintily. If you could see this middle-aged, never-smiling, spotless woman and the manifold ways she contrives for guarding us, you would be amused and touched. She seems to love us, at least to regard us as a pair of babes to be cared for.

We give some hours to study in the morning, then in the middle of the day go out, and are generally at home again an hour before dinner. In the evening we read aloud. You can imagine our delightful days in the Louvre, on the broad walks of St. Cloud, or under the trees and along the terrace of St. Germain. Whether on the Boulevards, or on the river, in the churches, shops, theatres, or restaurants, we are always in the midst of these throngs of merry pleasure-loving French people. They impress me as grown-up children who want pretty things and "a good time," but are far more thoughtless than intentionally wicked — as the Puritan regards them. And to be amused is not the only interest of the Paris of to-day. These people are wildly democratic. "Equality" is a passion with them. The kitchen maid respectfully addresses the young fellow who brings up the coal as "Monsieur." Everywhere and in every relation of life this love of equality occurs. The old fruit-woman at the corner expects and receives the same civility that belongs to "Madame." The rich and the poor are found together in their pleasures, and taking far more pleasure than with us, I am sure. Good nature and politeness are everywhere; yet when they give way, a Frenchman is capable of more brutality, I think, than any other human being.

But no one can realize who does not live here how

every man, woman, and child hates Germany. When we asked for Jaeger flannels the other day, the clerk declared that the French did not need German clothes. You insult a person by inquiring, even in the mildest way, if he speaks German. The History which the minister of education approves for French schools closes with an appeal to the boys to be soldiers and prepare to fight Germany, and to the girls to maintain the same "patriotism." In our peaceful parlor we hear the nightly cheers for Boulanger, who lives only a few doors away. Nobody can tell why he is so popular, except that he is "brave" and does n't like things as they are. The French must have somebody to adore, like a sentimental schoolgirl. Indeed how these Europeans, in the mass, like to be managed and governed!

Last week the weather was so fine we took three days in Picardy. We rode seventy-five miles on our bicycles, one hundred and eighty on the railroad. For cathedrals we saw Beaumont, Senlis, Noyon, Soissons, Laon; and for castles, Chantilly, Compiègne, Coucy, and Pierrefonds. Oh, such delicious country, full of happy harvesters! It is pure joy to ride through the rich fields. How pleasant to be so independent of trains, to be able to take thirty miles a day of glorious motion, seeing these beautiful scenes where world-influencing dramas have been played! We often long to make a present of the day we are enjoying to some one across the sea.

The chief crop of these central plains at present is sugar beets. They are enormous, and the farmers draw them on gigantic wagons with six white oxen to the factories. Men, women, and children are everywhere in the fields together, digging the beets, burning the tops, and making holiday. When we were riding before, the most striking thing was the ripe buckwheat. Now the beets take their turn, and of course great quantities of apples, potatoes, and carrots. I wish you could see the big oxen and the stout Normandy and Percheron horses. We stopped at the castle where the villain lived whose wickedness gave rise to the story of Blue-Beard. You will be relieved to know that at last he was hung for his cruelties.

Our Boston paper says that Catharine S. has married Mr. T. And who is Mr. T., and is it true? If it is true, I am glad for her with all my heart. Her health will be better and her writing less nervous, if once she is taken care of as you and I are so happily. Yes, my dear, I will confess that your husband is the best man in the world, except one. But I don't know what will happen if life goes on growing so much better and brighter each year. How does your cup manage to hold so much? Mine is running over, and I keep getting larger cups; but I can't contain all my blessings and gladness. We are both so well and busy that the days are never half long enough.

Thursday afternoon we left Avignon, where we had a week of great enjoyment. John Stuart Mill and his wife are buried there, and her daughter — now a woman of sixty — still lives in their house. I went to see her. A friend of hers, too, took me to meet some of the Provençal poets, so I drank tea in a palace built before 1400, where to-day an American lady lives whose daughter has married a marquis. We had much talk of America. The little daughter of the marquis sat in my lap and said she would go home with me "where the children play in English." I visited three girls' schools in Avignon, and for the first time in my life got into a convent school. The one for poor children was delightful; over three hundred little things under seven years of age, the sisters devoting themselves to them without pay. But the other, for the daughters of the aristocracy, was very fashionable, the teaching poor, and no discipline.

After Avignon and a day spent in Marseilles, we went by train as far as Fréjus. Since then we have been riding our bicycles along the Corniche Road, nearly two hundred miles. Every inch of it has been bliss, even the walk of twelve miles one day, pushing our bicycles up hill. One night we ran into this queer little Italian town of Alassio, nestling between the mountains and the sea, and found ourselves on a noble bay, sheltered on every side, and in a hotel which was a convent until five years ago. Our room is the chapel, still keeping its sacred decorations and its two long windows overlooking the unbroken sea, which rolls within twenty feet of our sunny balcony. All is so bewitching that instead of going the next morning, as we intended, we have remained five days, though we have only the clothes we carry on our bicycles. We lie in the sand, we gather the blossoming flowers, the ripe oranges and olives, and are sure that it is June and not January. Anything like this I have never experienced before, and I find it unspeakably fascinating. Indeed the whole Corniche Road is enchanting, with its perpetual roses, its palms loaded with ripening dates, and the blue sea under a cloudless sky. You two must certainly do it sometime. Married lovers could n't find a prettier holiday.

Here we are in Venice looking out on the Adriatic Sea, where the sun is setting like a great ball of fire that almost blinds my eyes when I lift them. All the morning that sun has been streaming into our two pretty rooms. We are having delicious weather, clear and soft, like a fresh Spring day at home. We sit in the sunshine, or wander up and down the narrow passage-ways, or float in fascinating gondolas, to our hearts' content. Just under our windows, so close that we see nothing between, lie rows upon rows of vessels. Forests of masts fly all flags that Webster's Dictionary knows and many others one imagines. Beyond these lie ocean steamers, and then the great and wide sea. I never felt so much abroad before. This melancholy mermaid city seems nothing short of a miracle; for as the eye rests on the salt green water stretching in every direction, it is impossible to feel that it is really shallow. Lately a road has been carried over half a mile of water to the mainland. As we stepped from the train it was perplexing to find myself in a great city, yet with no sound of horse, carriage, or any of the multitude of street noises which we usually associate with city life. The cabs are black gondolas, half way between a canoe and a Wellesley boat, and on them stands the picturesque Italian with his one oar, steering swiftly around sharp corners and under low bridges which cross the narrow spaces between high buildings on either side. It is altogether unreal. At present we are devoting much time to Italian. Last week we read together an Italian book of two hundred and fifty pages; and in odds and ends of time I have read in English Ruskin's "Stones of Venice," Howells'

"Venetian Life," Sismondi's "Italy," and am half through one of Symonds' books on the Renaissance. It is good to read the great books about Italy while among the scenes they discuss. How hard it will be some day to break away from the palace where we live and from the daily sight of the most beautiful church and the most beautiful pictures that the world contains! We know we ought to go south. But a spell is on us. There is always another picture to see of Titian or Veronese or Tintoret or Bellini or Carpaccio, and we linger.

Mother, dear, if my memory serves me, something important in the history of our family happened on this day thirty-five years ago. I think I cannot be mistaken in fixing so fundamental a date, though you may have been too youthful to retain a distinct recollection of the event. But I who profited by that marriage more than any one else, by at least twenty-one months, am heartily grateful to you for doing it, and send my congratulations on the day.

We are keeping the festival in royal fashion, spending the perfect Spring day in the country at Hadrian's Villa and Tivoli. All the superb morning we have been driving among the hills and valleys and olive-slopes and vineyards, seeing snowy mountains, rivers, city, and plain, with now and then a Robbia in a country church or an old convent fresco. The Sabine

Mountains are on one side of us, the Alban Hills on the other, and our road of twenty miles runs through fresh green fields. Mr. and Mrs. P. have been with us — he a writer, she an artist — and Mr. E. too, who is an intimate friend of Cardinal Hohenlohe. This Cardinal owns the beautiful Villa d' Este, and our sculptor took us through its stately rooms and its fascinating gardens. There we heard the nightingales, singing among cypresses that are many centuries old. The whole day has been a dream of delight, one of the most interesting since we came abroad — high praise indeed!

We have been in Rome several weeks and have given up practically all our time to sightseeing, something which we never intend to do. G. declares that he is ashamed of having seen so many things. We always try to keep half our day for study and home, and I am sure that in this way we gain more than the sightseers. But somehow in Rome every one catches the fever, and the number of wretched old ruins and scandalously tawdry and dirty churches that one can manage to gaze at and pry about is amazing; and all this fuss because here some old Roman set up a column to commemorate his brutal battles, or there some saint is imagined to have caused a spring of oil to burst from the stones, or to have walked about with his head in his hands among the soldiers who cut it off. But we have seen so many bones of saints and martyrs that we are now too hardhearted any longer to glance their way.

While our bicycles are being passed from one country to the other, I sit on a stone by the roadside and write to you. The whole population of the village is assembled to see what a lady with a bicycle can mean; and all the people are tipping my saddle and wondering over the cyclometer, astonished that such a little thing can measure distance. It really tells us that we have ridden more than a thousand miles already in France and Italy. We are now on our way from Venice to Vienna. We ride about thirty-five miles a day. Tuesday we were on the wide plain of Northern Italy and visited Asolo, the poet Browning's last country home. We saw his house and garden. In the Italian towns we came upon many splendid pictures. Yesterday we reached the mountain chain which divides Italy from Austria, and ever since have been climbing up or running down hills, following the beds of narrow streams which cut their way down snow-peaked mountains. The streams are very full, and the sound of mountain torrents is always with us. It is a strange, wild country, strange people too, so excited at seeing me on a bicycle that the town hurries to watch us pass. As we fly by, the women drop their baskets, cross themselves, and lift their hands, crying, "O Madonna mia!" G. says it is the greeting of "the new woman" by the old, and "the new" does n't even stop to listen.

But I must tell you how we are crossing the frontier. A little river separates the two countries, with Pontrebba on the Italian, and Pontafel on the Austrian side. Both ends of the bridge are guarded by three tremendous officials, each in the uniform of his native land, the two sets within easy talking distance. We rode up to the three Italians, dismounted, and presented our paper asking for the eighty-five francs exacted on our bicycles when we entered Italy, and destined to be returned when we depart. You would suppose no event of similar consequence had occurred in a century. It is impossible to report the consultations, the expeditions to other parts of the town, the hunting up of dignitaries that followed. An Austrian was finally summoned from his end of the bridge, the chief Italian swung a gun over his shoulder, and we were led across half a mile to the Austrian Custom House, where our bicycles were deposited, probably to make sure they would be out of Italy when we received our money. We ourselves returned in procession to Italy, our hands full of documents, and even then had to go to two other places before the money was paid. We reached the bridge at 9.30, and are just leaving it at 12.15. Our Italian chief would not attend to anything for half an hour, "because the train would pass then," so we were obliged to sit and meditate until that event occurred. Fancy these people in Chicago! Nirvana is the only place where they will feel really at home. But nothing can stop the delight of the day. It is very early Spring. The cuckoos are calling, the cherry trees are in blossom, and the grass is at its greenest. Here we leave dear Italy and must begin at once to limber up our German tongues. One of those words makes such a big mouthful that I choke and sneeze in spite of myself.

XI

CAMBRIDGE

On leaving Wellesley Mrs. Palmer had her first opportunity to become a lady of leisure. Up to this time she had been steadily under compulsion. The desire for education, the need of earning her own support, the demands of schools or the college with which she was connected, laid their necessitating hands upon her successive years and allowed her little freedom of choice. Now such severities were ended. She was to live in comfort, surrounded by all the opportunities for study, society, and travel which were especially congenial to her. Official ties were snapped. She had performed a difficult public work, climbing through it from obscurity to note, and she was still but thirty-two. For most of us at that age the tasks of life lie directly ahead; for Mrs. Palmer they were already behind.

And a lady of leisure of a peculiar sort Mrs. Palmer actually became. Henceforth she did what she pleased. I have called this last period of her career her time of Self-Expression, because all that was done in it sprang from the glad prompting of disciplined powers rather than from any pressure of out-

11 QUINCY STREET, CAMBRIDGE

ward obligation. Her times were in her hand; her own interests she was free to follow. This portion of my book will show how she followed them. Profoundly dear as they were, of course she followed them with energy, and even allowed them to make the fourth period of her life as active as the third. But it was a voluntary and exultant activity. Whoever saw her during these years remarked in her new buoyancy and a wider power. The shelter of a home had enlarged her scope. From special labor in a particular spot she advanced to general influence in the whole field of girls' education. The occupations of her thirteen winters in Cambridge I relate here, but I give them in a classified summary rather than in detailed chronological sequence.

Underneath them all ran a rich domestic life, though several years passed after Mrs. Palmer's marriage before she acquired a permanent and adequate home. That is something hard to find in Cambridge. The University occupies the centre of the town. Around it gather shops, churches, factories, stables, lodging houses; but the number of private dwellings is small. Whoever possesses one in the college neighborhood does not readily part with it. Those who connect themselves with the University for the first time have ordinarily an uncomfortable preliminary season, during which they sit at a distance, like fishhawks on a tree, spying after something to seize. On the whole, we passed this awkward period more easily than most of our colleagues. Between the wedding and the departure for Europe there were but six months. During these, and for a year after our return, we took houses already furnished on Broadway and Brattle Streets. Then for three years we occupied the Deanery of the Episcopal Theological School, until in 1894 we established ourselves in the historic house at the corner of the College Yard and Quincy Street. This house, built about 1815, was bought by the College twenty years later, was equipped as an observatory, and made the residence of its first Professor of Astronomy. Later it was occupied successively by President Felton, Bishop Huntington, and for thirty-three years by the saintly Dr. Andrew Preston Peabody. We readjusted its interior to our needs, constructing a large library and arranging Mrs. Palmer's study and waiting rooms so that in receiving one caller she need not be disturbed by the coming of another. To this house she became strongly attached. In it her complex work was done with the utmost convenience; here she easily assembled several hundred guests; its plain old-fashioned comfort made shy students feel at home; and it was but fifteen minutes distant from those parts of Boston to which business called her oftenest. An old house harbors peace better than a new one. At 11 Quincy Street Mrs. Palmer found that peace, found too the dignified surroundings to which her idealizing affections most naturally clung. Nearly half her life had been passed within college walls, until the august connection had become almost a part of her being. Here, among the buildings, trees, and grounds of our stateliest university that tie continued, but in a form which freed it from all burdensome responsibility.

When she left Wellesley I wondered how the business of housekeeping would suit her. Few young married women have had so little experience of it. For fifteen years, almost uninterruptedly since she left her early home, she had been an inmate of some sort of institution, where attention to the daily bread had been the charge of some other person than herself. Her rooms were generally already prepared, and the care of them, with the heating and lighting, was delegated to an official. Her special occupations were as remote as possible from such affairs. Indeed in these matters I was more experienced than she, having managed my own home for the nine preceding years and become somewhat proficient in the simpler forms of cookery. Whether rivalry with my accomplishments stimulated her, or whether success here was simply another instance of that versatility which usually enabled her to do with instantaneous excellence whatever she was called to do, I cannot say; but certainly almost from the beginning she showed herself the skilful mistress of her household. She was about as often consulted by bewildered housekeepers on puddings, carpets, and servants, as by teachers in regard to situations and text-books. In all things an artist, she prided herself on the beauty and orderliness of her home and was constantly studying how more intelligence might be brought into domestic methods. A few details in regard to the daily conduct of that home will picture her housewifery.

From the first she was our financial manager. Whatever money was received by either of us was put into her safe-keeping; and it was she who then appropriately distributed it to tradesmen, pockets, and banks. The skilful planning of how to extract the largest enjoyment from a given outlay was a game she delighted to play, and I think her favorite volume was her classified account book. Her table, while offering few articles at a meal, must have these exquisitely cooked and widely varied from day to day. Her rooms must each have their distinctive note; in those used chiefly by herself were gathered mementoes of her childhood and the faces of those with whom she had since been associated. Seldom did she order a hat or dress outright; she would choose good stuffs, but must give them her own individual touch. Her wardrobe, therefore, most expressive of herself, cost her incredibly little; she ever setting taste above expenditure, and often quoting in this connection the lines of an old poet, —

> Say not then this with that lace will do well,
> But this with my discretion will be brave.

In servants she was insistent on personal quality, preferring the capable green girl to the one who already "knew it all." Such a one she would quickly attach, carefully train, and then trust with large responsibility. Each servant must have a room of her own, be treated as a member of the household, and be allowed to go and come at her own discretion, provided always that her work was exactly performed. Mutual consideration was soon established; and though Mrs. Palmer paid no excessive wages, she was a stranger to "the servant problem." One servant was with her for ten years and others for periods approximately long.

In all this domestic side of life she took great pleasure, becoming a joyous expert not merely in that cheap thing "domestic science," but in the subtler matters of domestic art. Powers trained elsewhere were quickly adjusted to the home and used for the comfort of those she loved. When at one time she was struggling with a new cook on the subject of bad bread, and after encountering the usual excuses of oven, flour, and yeast, had invaded the kitchen and herself produced an excellent loaf, astonished Bridget summed up the situation in an epigram which deserves to be recorded: "That's what education means — to be able to do what you've never done before."

Naturally, having created so beautiful a home, she used it liberally for entertainment, though no sharp distinction was ever drawn between entertainment and business. Three children of friends were with us for more than a year each, and almost every meal had also its interesting guest. With most of the colleges of the country she had some connection; and no week in the year passes without a wanderer from one of them appearing in Cambridge. Generally he appeared at her table, with no great pressure was induced to spend the night, and then what detailed and eager talk was heard about the policies and prospects of his college! What feasible proposals she would offer for its strengthening! How fitted to their surroundings were the candidates she named for its instructors! Her hospitable mind admitted no notion of colleges as rivals; all were alike members of the one army of education. At other meals appeared the young women whose opening fortunes required an assisting hand. There came, too, directors of her many societies and the members of innumerable committees. Poor people came, whose only reason for coming was hopelessness. And here also gathered her host of personal friends, eager always to gaze, to listen, and to be quickened. Often of an evening, and always on Tuesday and Sunday afternoons, there were Harvard students, some bringing notes of introduction, some already counting themselves her children, and easily getting their slender claims acknowledged. With them all she talked much, gaily or gravely, as occasion required. By turns she was suggestive, inspiring, consolatory, or simply amusing; ever light of touch, ready of anecdote, charming all and setting all at ease, while the plainest fact was not allowed to pass without some shining word, or the merriest jest without its hold on reality. This perpetual mingling of sobriety and play was hers from childhood. I was often reminded of Shenstone's heroine: —

> With her mien she enamors the brave;
> With her wit she engages the free;
> With her modesty pleases the grave;
> She is every way pleasing to me.

Of her relations with my own work I may say that while she assisted me in making acquaintance with my students and had much influence over student life in general, for philosophy itself she had no natural inclination, its speculative side being peculiarly foreign to her. She was a woman of action, ideals, and practical adjustments. But none the less she honored what she did not herself pursue, and felt strongly the vital issues of the ethical doctrines which it was mine to elaborate. With full understanding and sympathy she discussed the less technical parts of my studies and offered her mind as a field for experimentation. Whatever I wrote was submitted to her exacting taste. But in all our intellectual companionship there was no merging; each had his and her special interests, to which the other came merely as a novice. I was as ignorant of her school problems and of what was being done for the training of girls as she of my dialectics. Her style of speech and writing remained her own, widely unlike mine. We prized the strength of difference rather than that of identity, though pleased at any parts within us which happened to be interchangeable. Usually she took charge of the kitchen, and I of the college; but when she was called for a time to Chicago or elsewhere to manage a college, she left the kitchen to me. If one of us had promised a public address and was suddenly disabled, the other appeared. Contrasted and supplemental occupations, profound sympathy, and occasional substitutions formed our happy bond. St. Paul says that "love envieth not," but is glad when the loved one possesses what he lacks.

In describing the activities of her winter months I linger long over the home and its habits, because in her judgment — and in that also, I believe, of those who knew her best — the roots of her power were there. People sometimes spoke of her as a "public character," not noticing how the phrase — though true — blots what was most distinctive of her. Her publicity was but an expression of her private womanhood. She was the same person everywhere. Led by broad popular sympathies to improve the conditions of her sex, she preserved in a public field the simplicity, ease, dignity, and refinement which graced her fireside. She did not turn to occupations outside the home because those within it were distasteful; but powers already exceptional when she entered that home became there so refreshed, gladdened, and enlarged that they overflowed the usual bounds and ran forth in multitudinous blessing. I have said in discussing our marriage that something of this sort was from the first our hope. And so it proved. The work begun at Wellesley was not broken during the fifteen years in Cambridge, but was vastly assisted by the surroundings of a home. What was that work? Was it as fragmentary as it sometimes seemed, or had it inner unity and a ground in public needs? Before marking out its several sections, it will be well to fix attention for a moment on its genuine unity.

The times were critical when Mrs. Palmer appeared. Social transformations were in progress. Girls were just emerging from sheltered homes, desirous of education and of whatever else might help to enlarge their lives. Many feared that such desires might dispose them to drop the quietness, delicacy, and spiritual power which were hereditarily theirs and to admit into their natures the ruder forces of our turbulent world. Most social changes involve danger. Mrs. Palmer did much to lessen this danger and to quiet these fears. She not only opened college doors, but she helped to fix a standard of what college girls should be. Persuasively and in her own person she showed how a deepened intelligence and a wider knowledge of affairs may heighten the characteristic and ancestral traits of woman and permanently increase her charm. Each of Mrs. Palmer's undertakings in this her culminating period represents a single aspect of the one aim, to guide the emancipation and integrity of women, particularly as these are affected by education. A priestly and impalpable task it was, to become the watcher of a social transition; but it was an immensely important task, and one for which she was singularly fitted. The several forms which this aim assumed I now describe.

In the first place she kept her allegiance to Wellesley, and to it gave a large amount of time. That college is governed by a large Board of Trustees, but its immediate direction is in the hands of the President and a small Executive Committee. On this committee Mrs. Palmer accepted a place, and was seldom absent from its meetings. She had her distinct lines of policy there, but in working with others it was her habit rather to inspire than to dictate. She would open up a subject, state the facts, explain the principles involved, draw attention to the essential features of the case, and wait for others to offer their opinions. By conviction she was patient of debate, believing that no matter is ever really settled till all its points are discussed. When a decision was to be reached, she liked better to have it brought about by the judgment of others than through her advocacy. In deliberations with her one got the impression of a person who has no way of her own, but who merely joins with others in a common search for the best way.

Such a spirit of moderation, tact, and respect for dissenting opinions was peculiarly needed on the Wellesley committee during her membership; for the college was then passing through grave transitions. Three presidents came successively into office, all strong and independent women, much unlike herself, all chosen with her approval and ever her constant friends. Then certain arrangements of the college made by its founders underwent considerable change. Mr. and Mrs. Durant had established and highly valued a low tuition fee, a system of daily domestic work, "Silent Times," and frequent attendance on religious exercises. As the college grew, these provisions conflicted with more important interests and were one after the other removed. But much time and mutual forbearance were needed for changes so fundamental. Mrs. Palmer favored them all, working toward them in company with Mrs. Durant — the sturdy defender of her husband's plans so long as defence was likely to effect anything; but who, when the new order was established, showed herself as loyal to it as to the old. During this period, too, it became necessary to find a new treasurer, to adopt a new system of financial control and report, and in general to transfer the college from private to public guardianship. All this the Trustees would have found impossible without the coöperation and magnanimity of Mrs. Durant; but under the best of circumstances it brought on them, and especially on the executive committee, a burdensome amount of care. Of this care Mrs. Palmer took her full share, as she did also of the selection of teachers, the assistance of poor students, and the raising of funds both for them and for the many needs of the expanding college. Whatever helps a girls' college she believed helps men and women everywhere.

She was consequently ready to aid other colleges beside Wellesley. In 1892 the University of Chicago was founded and called us to two of its chairs; she to be Professor of History and Dean of Women, I to be the head of the department of Philosophy. It was an attractive offer. Here once more pioneer work gave opportunity for that creative power in which she had already proved herself strong. Most of those engaged in organizing the novel university she knew well, and many of its Faculty were her personal friends. She admired the wisdom of its chief founder, who accepted no place on its Board of Trustees, selected or rejected none of its teachers, gave no money to its buildings, but provided liberal means for carrying on a university so far as others might come forward to construct it. Of course she approved the provision of its constitution which opens to women as well as men all its opportunities of study and teaching; for in her judgment, and in mine too, coeducation is the goal at which all colleges must ultimately arrive. Yet in spite of these attractions, and the fact that the salaries offered were three times what we then received in Cambridge, her voice was from the first against accepting the calls. She loved her home. She cared little for money, having modest tastes and much enjoyment, as I have already shown, in getting large results from small outlays. My roots, she thought, were too deep in Harvard soil for removal to be quite honorable. She doubted whether our scholarly opportunities in Chicago would equal those in Cambridge, did not like to interpose such a distance between herself and Wellesley, and perhaps dreaded the wear and tear to which she would be exposed by another absorption in college duties. We accordingly declined the call.

But President Harper was insistent. Founding for the first time a great coeducational university in a city, he desired Mrs. Palmer's planning and superintendence, even if she were not to be continuously on the ground. He proposed, therefore, that she should accept the Deanship of Women, without teaching, and with no obligation to reside in Chicago more than twelve weeks. The periods of her residence might be distributed throughout the year according to her convenience. In fact they often fell in times of my recesses, when we could be in Chicago together. She was to have general superintendence of the women's lodging, food, conduct, and choice of studies, and to select a sub-Dean to carry on the work in her absence. This proposal she accepted for the year 1892–93, and then, finding that measures well begun grow strong only by watching, she somewhat unwillingly allowed herself to continue two years more. By that time the position of the women students was assured. They were certain to hold a place in the university no less creditable than that of the men. There was no need of her difficult service. In June, 1895, she resigned, had a successor appointed, and sailed away to Europe. But her interest in the university never ceased, nor did its gratitude to her. A group of its friends have recently set a chime of bells in its tower, forever to voice her praise.

Wellesley and Chicago, however, were not the only colleges of her care. Divergent Radcliffe was coming into existence beside her door. For a dozen years, through a Society for the Collegiate Instruction of Women, girls had been obtaining more or less teaching from Harvard professors. In 1894 the Massachusetts Legislature was asked to transform this Society into Radcliffe College, to grant its students degrees, and formally to attach it to Harvard University. In this movement Mrs. Palmer took an active interest. It is true she thought the coeducational and the separate colleges for women have advantages superior to anything the segregated type can offer. Possibly those who devised the plan of segregation were more concerned with guarding men's colleges from change than with enlarging woman's opportunities. Evidently too this subordinated arrangement obliges women to seat themselves, as it were, at a second table, where the intellectual food is merely such surplus as is not needed elsewhere. Mrs. Palmer, at least, did not conceal from herself that such a college must always live on favors, not on rights, that the greater part of its instruction is likely to fall into young and inexperienced hands, and that when its teachers are pressed for time they will withdraw from its service and attend to the superior claims of the men. But these inherent weaknesses did not discourage her hopeful spirit. She was confident that whatever errors the plan contained would in time be disclosed and amended. She trusted Harvard scholarship, she wished to extend its influence, and she thought that even a second table in Cambridge must prove invigorating to hungry girls. She saw too how in a transitional season like ours, when parents are slowly discovering that knowledge harms girls as little as boys, it is well to have that knowledge offered in as wide a variety of forms as possible. The very differences therefore between Radcliffe and the other colleges commended the experiment to her support.

In connecting the new college with Harvard the question arose whether degrees should be given by Harvard itself or by Radcliffe. Persons whose chief interest was the education of women favored the former; those who were primarily solicitous for Harvard, the latter scheme. It soon became plain that Harvard must decline to give the degrees unless Radcliffe possessed at the start an endowment of not less than $100,000. Whether they would be given even then could not be determined until the Spring meeting of the Harvard Corporation. In the mean time the Woman's Education Association of Boston, of which Mrs. Palmer was president, took up the matter of endowment with enthusiasm, appointing her chairman of a small committee charged to raise the contemplated sum. To this endeavor her winter of 1893–94 was largely given. By letters, by arranged interviews, and most of all by personal solicitation she, in company with a friend or two, canvassed Boston and many more distant places. Persuasions of hers were never easy to resist, and before the end of the winter she had obtained over $90,000. When, however, the question came before the Harvard Corporation, they decided by a majority of one to require Radcliffe to give its own degrees, President Eliot favoring the opposite policy. The money raised by Mrs. Palmer was accordingly returned to the subscribers. A few years later she aided in raising $110,000 for Wellesley.

Having so strong an interest in every type of women's college, Mrs. Palmer naturally gave much time to fostering the Collegiate Alumnæ Association. This is a league of women graduated from the better colleges throughout the country, who are banded together for educational and friendly purposes. It seeks to sort the colleges which are open to women, to fix standards of excellence, and to bring pressure to bear on those of a low order and induce them to raise their requirements. No college is admitted to membership which does not reach a certain grade in entrance examinations, in number and efficiency of teachers, in size of endowment and library, and in conditions for the Bachelor's degree. The certificate of membership consequently becomes proof that its holder is a student of sound training. It is accepted at the universities both of this country and Europe, and admits a woman to higher study without further examination. Mrs. Palmer was one of the original organizers of this association, and one of its early presidents. Throughout her life she attended its meetings and served on its two laborious committees, the committee on membership and the committee on foreign fellowships; the length of her many terms of service in its various offices, if added together, aggregating fifty-three years. Foreign fellowships she felt to be matters of such importance that she spent much time in sifting the candidates, corresponded with them while they were abroad, and often raised considerable sums for their support. Since her death a fellowship of this sort has been founded in her name by the Collegiate Alumnæ Association; and another, also called by her name and yielding an income of $1000, has been put in charge of Wellesley College.

I have mentioned the Woman's Education Association, a hard-working body to which Mrs. Palmer gave many years of fruitful service. Certain public-spirited ladies of Boston had banded themselves together "to promote the better education of women." By this phrase they meant not the support of educational agencies already established, but the more difficult business of watchfulness, invention, and experiment. It was theirs to initiate movements, to finance them for a time, testing them carefully; and then when they were proved to have worth, to turn them over to independent organizations. In this way they opened opportunities to women in many directions previously unthought of. Under their charge and at their cost Harvard University was induced to conduct a series of examinations for girls graduating from preparatory and high schools, examinations which were afterwards put in charge of Radcliffe College. For them the Massachusetts Institute of Technology opened its chemical laboratories. They aided the study of biology by providing means for seaside summer work, out of which germ was developed the important marine station at Wood's Hole. To them too were due the beginnings of the training of district nurses, the study of home economics, the diet kitchen, emergency lectures, sloyd, travelling libraries. They founded foreign fellowships, looked after city schools, the vacations of working girls, the poor, the deaf, the trees on Boston Common — in short interested themselves in all those matters where women's watchfulness can increase the intelligence, beauty, and dignity of a city.

In 1891 this society had fallen into decay. Its

meetings were slenderly attended and the question of disbanding arose. Finally it was decided to continue if Mrs. Palmer would accept the presidency. It was usually her habit to listen too readily to calls of this sort, and mine to be fierce in opposition. Her kind heart was so easily solicited that for her protection a certain savagery was sometimes necessary. But in this case our parts were reversed. I saw in the society a power which, if properly directed, might produce much; but she proved strangely obdurate. By degrees it appeared that, while she did not know these ladies, she imagined them rich, cold, and fashionable, likely to be alarmed over woman suffrage and coeducation, "not at all her kind." She, a Western girl, could never work well with people of that sort, she said, nor could they possibly have any liking for her.

I hardly know how she came at last to accept their presidency for a single year; but once in, she was unanimously reëlected in nine successive years. She herself soon discovered her mistaken estimate, and nowhere did she ever find a company more loyal or congenial. The Association sprang into vigorous life. Its membership enormously increased, its meetings were largely attended; and while wide differences of opinion continued among its members over the proper scope of woman's activity, all shades of belief were respected and its committees aided pretty diverse causes. Where Mrs. Palmer was, quarrelling was usually difficult, frankness and mutual consideration easy. But she worked hard. I find in her notebooks memoranda of six public meetings and six executive committee meetings a winter, at all of which she presided. For the public meetings subjects must be selected and notable speakers obtained. And though no one could have been more efficiently supported than she, it was inevitable that much of the care of planning the varied work of the Association should fall upon her. The year before she went abroad for the last time, she insisted on her resignation being accepted, for she did not think it well that a society should be too long under a single leader.

And since in passing I have mentioned woman's suffrage, perhaps I shall save Mrs. Palmer from misconception if I indicate more precisely her attitude toward that heated question. Both she and I were members of the Equal Suffrage Association and had no doubt that eventually women will vote as naturally and with as little disturbance to the community as do men. She knew many of the leading suffragists and admired them for their refinement, their patience, and their readiness to bear abuse in the public interest. Such dispositions she counted admirably feminine. Whenever she came home after meeting sensible Mary Livermore, or sweet-voiced

Lucy Stone, or perpetually youthful Julia Ward Howe, a new nobility seemed communicated to herself. Yet she did not appear on their platforms nor press the legislature to grant their great request. While never concealing her sympathies, and agreeing with a remark made to her by Phillips Brooks, that "it frightened him to see what civic government had come to, unaided by women," she felt that the movement toward suffrage was advancing with great — perhaps with sufficient — rapidity. She was eager, before it reached its conclusion, to give women juster minds, sounder bodies, more equable nerves, and a clearer consciousness of themselves as something more than pretty creatures of society. These were the important matters; suffrage but an auxiliary, though worthy, crown. It could wait, they could not. Then too these were the interests specifically intrusted to her, and into the furtherance of them she threw herself with a whole-hearted zeal which was not easily diverted to side issues.

THE LIBRARY AT 11 QUINCY STREET

XII

CAMBRIDGE (CONTINUED)

In 1889 Mrs. Palmer was appointed by Governor Ames a member of the Massachusetts State Board of Education. This position she held during the remaining thirteen years of her life, being reappointed by Governor Greenhalge and Governor Crane, until she became the senior member of the Board. The Board consists of eight members and has direct control of the normal schools only; but indirectly and through oversight it influences all the public instruction of the state. At its instance new legislation is initiated or, still more important, prevented. In the annual report of its secretary statistics of the schools are given and their condition elaborately set forth. It employs half a dozen agents to visit the schools of the isolated sections, to learn about their strength and weakness, and to give friendly advice to the teachers. Under their direction some twenty-five Teachers' Institutes, a sort of migratory normal school, are held each year. At these the teachers of the country towns, for the most part women, assemble for acquaintance, criticism, and guidance. Long regular meetings of the Board are held each month; special meetings as often as business requires.

To this oversight of the public schools Mrs. Palmer devoted an incalculable amount of time, tact, and experience. She visited, corresponded, interviewed, served on committees, appealed to the legislature, and with such success that at her death the normal schools, and to a great extent the country schools also, had been reorganized and brought to an efficiency unknown before. In 1902 the Secretary of the Board could truthfully write that "in qualifications for admission to its normal schools no state has yet adopted standards so high or so satisfactory."

No one would profess that these important changes were due to Mrs. Palmer alone. That was seldom true of any of her undertakings. I have a constant difficulty in narrating what she did, because it is always tangled with what others did and cannot be separately assessed. From the beginning her public career was one of association and of work accomplished in groups. Nothing pleased her more than so to escape observation and, while giving of her best, to have it merged in the indistinguishable best of others. On the State Board too she found strong colleagues and a ready spirit of coöperation. My only method therefore of describing this laborious section of her life is to set down the improvements in the schools which were effected during her term of office, and to say that in these improvements her prudent mind, persuasive tongue, and resourceful courage bore no inconsiderable part.

During her time the Massachusetts Normal Schools were increased from six to ten, and all the original six were equipped with new buildings. To get the bills passed, locations selected, plans of buildings drawn and executed for ten great plants, is no slight job. Faithfulness in public service involves a good many plodding hours. But the internal reconstruction was more significant still. Its successive steps were, I believe, the following. In 1893 the permanent Secretary of the Board — a devoted man, of some limitations, who had kept the old system steady for seventeen years — retired, and the earlier conception of a normal school as a place of general education which might well be substituted for the high school came to an end. Thenceforth only high school graduates were admitted to the normal schools, where they immediately began to devote themselves to professional study. Before, students had been allowed to end their work in winter or summer; for the future a single graduation in June was fixed, and the course was solidly organized with reference to a definite date. More careful examinations for entrance and graduation were established. The traditional period of study had been but two years. In 1897 the schools at which Mrs. Palmer was a visitor, Bridgewater and Hyannis, had both lengthened their courses, and in that year a general vote was passed permitting the visitors and principal of any normal school to add to its course a third year of study and practice. It will be understood too that these larger changes were accompanied by a multitude of impalpable ones, in short by a general elevation of scholarly ideals. And this spirit was the more readily brought about because of an excellent provision for personal contact which had always existed. By a rule of the Board each of its members has two schools under his or her immediate charge. These he is expected frequently to visit, to become acquainted with their needs and teachers, to preside at their graduations, and to write an annual report on their condition. Membership on the State Board of Education, though unpaid, is no sinecure.

I have said that the Board did not confine itself to normal schools. In the year that Mrs. Palmer joined it a bill was passed encouraging the employment by all country schools of superintendents instead of local committees, allowing neighboring towns to combine in employing such a superintendent, and furnishing grants from the state treasury to meet part of the expense. A more important measure was carried in 1891 and greatly extended in 1894. This opened free high schools to our whole population, for it provided that a child in any town where there is no high school may claim free tuition at the school of a neighboring town. In 1894, too, examinations were established under the State Board to test the qualifications of candidates for teachers in the elementary schools. The following year manual training, of a type to be approved by the Board, was required in all high schools. The general aim of these changes was to put within the reach of the country child opportunities for development similar to those which the city child enjoys. In all this beneficent upbuilding of the schools Mrs. Palmer was a tireless worker. In view of what she did, her grateful colleagues have entered on their records the sense of loss her death occasioned to the Commonwealth and have added that always "her first concern was for the children of the state, that they should have the best facilities for the acquisition of knowledge, the training of their intellectual powers, and the development of their characters; her next was for the teachers, especially those in the humbler places, that everything should be done to make their calling comfortable and dignified. She was courageous before committees of the legislature in advocating the measures deemed wise by the Board and in seeking to avoid the evils of mischievous legislation." But how heavy a burden this work for the state laid on her will easily be understood.

It was during her membership on this board that she came forward in defence of the schools against improper temperance teaching. One of the more extreme temperance organizations attempted to put text-books into the schools which should paint the effects of alcohol in colors dark enough to terrify all users. Mrs. Palmer believed these books to be pleas, and not scientific statements. She thought them exaggerated, unfitted to train a child's sense of truth, and therefore unlikely in the long run to effect their purpose. With that purpose she was in hearty agreement. She believed it had been proved that alcohol is physically injurious; she knew that it had a closer alliance with human misery than any other agent known to man; and both she and her parents had long supported legal control of the traffic. Yet with her usual courage she faced misconception, led the State Board in opposing the measure, fought it for several weeks in legislative committees, and finally killed the bill. One of her colleagues has said, "She was the most persuasive debater I ever knew."

Much time during the winters of 1891 and 1892 was given to preparing for the Columbian Exposition at Chicago. To plan and conduct there an exhibit for Massachusetts a board of managers was appointed by the Governor, and of the five constituting it Mrs. Palmer was one. Several meetings of this board were held each month. There was a building to be constructed, exhibits to be gathered, loans of historical articles to be solicited, public interest to be aroused. The managers had the aid of a peculiarly efficient executive commissioner; but as Mrs. Palmer at this period was often in Chicago on university duty, no little responsibility at the fair grounds fell upon her. With the opening of the fair social functions began. Then too Massachusetts made education an important feature of its exhibit, and this required the special oversight of Mrs. Palmer. Partly through her influence the state collections on this subject were afterwards gathered into a permanent educational museum. On the whole, Massachusetts made an exceptionally complete and beautiful showing at the fair; but it was managed with such watchfulness and regard for public interests that at its close the managers were able to turn back into the state treasury more than a fifth of the not large appropriation voted by the legislature.

When the fair was projected many women's organizations throughout the country thought the occasion a favorable one for showing what had recently been accomplished by their neglected half of our race. They accordingly equipped a building with an excellent exhibit of the products of women's work, extending all the way from the nursery to the fine arts. But Mrs. Palmer did not join them. In her view the dignified position of man and woman is in comradeship, and not in places apart. She gladly saw the exhibits of Wellesley and Radcliffe installed beside those of the men's colleges, and took even more satisfaction in what the coeducational colleges could show.

To several other boards she gave brief terms of service. For many years she was one of the two hundred and fifty corporate members of the American Board of Commissioners for Foreign Missions, in company with only six other women. Soon after she came to Cambridge, she was made President of the Woman's Home Missionary Association and found in its wide affairs a happy blending of her religious, charitable, patriotic, and educational aims. Its work is largely among women and children. Into the outlying parts of our country, where agencies of civilization are few, it carries material aid, intellectual instruction, and divine hopes. Such a body needs from time to time the impulse of a fresh, though experienced, executive; and this it found in Mrs. Palmer. During her period of office contributions were increased and stolid audiences stirred to helpfulness by her moving accounts of hardship and heroism. But to remain at the head of this congenial organization would have removed her too far from the business of education for which she was specifically trained. She therefore held the presidency for only three years, remaining however a vice-president throughout her life. It was often her way, when she was unable to engage continuously in tasks which she counted important, to throw herself into them for a time and, after imparting her own enthusiasm and business methods to those about her, to leave on their hands the execution of what she had planned. Perhaps her most useful characteristic was this ability to inspire and to deputize.

When the war with Spain was over, a strangely friendly feeling toward that country appeared among our people. On our streets one could hardly say which was the more popular admiral, Dewey or Cervera. To show kindness where we had been obliged to use force, and to offer help to a nation trying to extricate itself from bonds of the past, was the desire of the hour. Everybody felt it. To the Cubans in 1900 Harvard opened freely its lecture rooms, and Mrs. Palmer her home. The sixteen Cuban girls who spent the summer there were under the charge of a remarkable woman, Mrs. Alice Gordon Gulick. After many years of work in Spain as a missionary, she had laid the foundations at San Sebastian of an International Institute designed to give Spanish girls such opportunity for advanced instruction as is offered in our colleges and academies. She knew very well that intellectual desires among women were as yet hardly astir in Spain, and that the work of awakening them would be a long one.

It was foreseen that most of the necessary funds must come from America. But Mrs. Gulick had much of Mrs. Palmer's patient and stimulating power, and already had made for herself something of a name in Spain. When the war was over the International Institute was reorganized, Mrs. Palmer becoming its president and Admiral Sampson one of its directors. Grounds and a building were obtained in Madrid, money for further development was solicited, the girls' colleges of this country were pledged to aid, and one or two slender classes were graduated. Just as the prospects of ultimate success were bright, Mrs. Palmer died, and her death was soon followed by that of Mrs. Gulick, exhausted in the cause. But enough had already been accomplished by these ardent women to mark the path along which others might safely carry onward the intended gift to Spain.

Not until the first half of the nineteenth century did it occur to Americans that girls as well as boys would profit by the higher education. Even then nothing so revolutionary as college training was planned; but a peculiar sort of advanced school, called a seminary or academy, began to appear in which it was sought to "finish" a girl by giving her just that amount of acquaintance with intellectual things which would quiet her mind without upsetting it, and without in any way damaging her attraction for man. One of the earliest and best of these venturesome schools was Bradford Academy, thirty miles from Boston, From 1804 to 1836 it admitted boys and girls; after 1836, girls only. For more than half a century it had an honorable career, but then declined until its numbers were insufficient to maintain its plant. Such schools almost inevitably move toward decay and by a kind of natural development tend to supersede themselves. The rising desire for knowledge which they meet and stimulate passes beyond them; and unless they are readjusted to modern conditions, they cease to hold the place in the community which was once rightfully theirs. Bradford reached such a crisis in 1900, when its despairing trustees turned to Mrs. Palmer. They wanted her to enter their board and join in an effort of resurrection. In view of the amount of her other work, she hesitated; but at last, finding that the first requisite for a successful school, a strong head, could not be had unless she became a trustee, she consented. For the two years before she died Bradford was one of her principal cares. During this time it passed from obscurity to a degree of public favor as great as it had ever known. Able men and women joined its board of trustees; its methods of study were modernized; its teachers were increased and their salaries raised; its debt was checked; it attracted as many students as its rooms could hold; and a way was prepared for the enlargement which has gone on since her death. In this case, as in many others, the remarkable results cannot be called hers. Many earnest men and women joined in producing them. But wherever she came, earnest men and women were pretty sure to appear and to find such success in their undertakings as they had previously believed impossible.

When I was in Venice in the summer of 1905, I needed help in a little Italian business. Learning that a certain lady might furnish it, I applied to her. She doubted if she had the necessary time. I pressed. Though she spoke no English, she said she had some acquaintance with America and began to inquire who I was. I reported myself a Harvard professor, but she remained obstinate. Incidentally I mentioned that my wife was formerly president of Wellesley College. Then all barriers went down. Was I the husband of Alice Freeman Palmer? She was adored in Italy. Poor Italians coming to America had been badly plundered. Attempts had been made in several cities to start a society for their protection, but with little success, until in Boston it had been suggested that Mrs. Palmer should head the movement. Then difficulties disappeared. I was obliged to say that I knew nothing of all this. Only two incidents connected with it could I subsequently recall. One day, in the year she went abroad for the last time, I picked up from her desk a circular appealing for the protection of Italian immigrants. Making some slurring remark about the absurdity of sending such things to an educational expert, I tossed the paper down. She was silent. A little later a letter came, addressed to her as president of the league for the protection of Italian immigrants. Then I broke into hot remonstrance. Was she, when already strained by Bradford and much else, so reckless as to go outside her province and take up something for which she had no special knowledge or fitness? She glanced up from her writing and gently said that I was taking things quite too seriously. She did not usually travel far from her own field, nor had she any idea now of giving important time to outside affairs. These people certainly were in a pitiful case, and some of her friends had asked her to lend her name for their aid. That was all. She might preside at a public meeting or two, but could give little further attention to the matter. She never mentioned the subject again. How much she may have done I do not know to-day. But three years after she had left our earth I came on the tracks of her quiet good deeds in far-away Venice.

Being known to have uncommon administrative talents and entire readiness to place them at the service of whoever needed them, she became during these years in Cambridge a kind of educational adviser. Schools and colleges all over the country turned to her in their perplexities, seldom in vain. She knew the right candidate to recommend for professor, dean, trustee, or even president, and she chose him with singular adaptation to his environment. In discussing problems of administration she was ingenious in suggestion, divining by a kind of instinct what would or would not work under the given circumstances. Only the circumstances must be actual, in order to bring out her best powers of judgment. Give her a theoretic problem in educational tactics, and you might find her uninterested and get a commonplace reply. But let her feel a living school or college in difficulty, and she would almost immediately perceive some shrewd way out. This dangerous sagacity overwhelmed her with correspondence, a correspondence so personal that she generally preferred to conduct it with her own pen. As soon as she entered the house she sat down at her desk, where she remained pretty steadily until summoned by callers. Calls of a formal sort she did not herself make, but only calls of business and occasionally of refreshment. During one of her busiest winters she spent half an hour each week with the two children of a Boston friend. Throwing herself on the floor, she built block houses with them, told stories, or dallied with Noah's Ark, until the clock announced a committee meeting. But calls on herself were regarded as even more sacred than letters. She reserved an afternoon a week for them, besides having them distributed through all other days. Nobody was dismissed briefly. By her fireside one got the impression that time was lazily abundant. I think she did not know a bore when she saw him — and she saw him under every guise. Sometimes he appeared as the crazy schemer, anxious to hitch his rickety wagon to her auspicious star. Even then, while protected by her own good sense, she would not damage that self-confidence which was his only possession. These direct contacts with persons through calls and letters she valued extremely; and large as was the draft they made on her time, they were probably worth while. To them she had been disciplined at Wellesley, and by them she recreated many a human soul.

I have said nothing about her public speeches, for the truth is I have rarely heard them. Whenever she spoke I was obliged to have an important engagement elsewhere. Her banishment of me was not through timidity, I think. Few speakers have so little of that. But in addressing an audience, she used to say, she must speak to all and not to any single one among them. Yet again and again some obscure person from her audience has told me that it seemed as if all she said was intended for him alone, such penetrating intimacy was in her words. Quietly they fell, as if in her own library; the simple language touched with a strange veracity, the clinging voice modulated so that the farthest auditor listened with pleasure; while the swift sentences unfolded her theme smoothly, tactfully, often humorously; anecdote, argument, home-thrust, or thrilling passage within easy command, and all welded together so solidly and with so little self-consciousness that at the close it seemed impossible to take any other view of the subject than the one presented. President Angell has said that "few speakers have in so large measure as she that magnetic unanalyzable power, divinely given now and then to some fortunate man or woman, of captivating and charming and holding complete possession of assemblies from the first to the last utterance."

Rarely was she fatigued while speaking. She was too much absorbed for that, and she followed what was said as eagerly as any who listened. But she ordinarily came home despondent. To my inquiry how things had gone, "Wretchedly," she would say. "Why did you let me accept that invitation?" And just before an address she was often equally downhearted. She would come hurrying into the house, saying she had a speech to make in Boston the next hour and nothing to make it of. What should she do? And how foolish she had been to promise it three months before! In later years these things gave me little alarm; for I found her speeches were not made *ex tempore*, but *ex omni tempore*, from a rich experience and with a delicate sense of literary form. Her best place for preparing them was on the street, in contact with people, and before an audience. But in the early years I did not understand these inspired processes, and thought my wooden ways universally applicable. Shortly after we married she had an address to make of more than usual importance. When the time was only a month distant, I asked if she had selected her subject? She said she should do so soon. After another fortnight I began to press on her the importance of making notes. But callers happened to be numerous just then and committees urgent. When but three more days were left, I became positively miserable and made her about equally so. She shut herself up in her room the last day and spent its wretched hours in fruitless meditation. I saw when she left me for the hall that she was thoroughly disorganized, and she told me — I believe truthfully — that she went to pieces on the platform. Several persons inquired of me what had been the matter that day with Mrs. Palmer. I knew too well: the trouble was meddling I. Henceforth I trusted her temperament, and I do not think she ever again made so bad a failure.

From her notebooks I learn that there were years in which these public addresses ran as high as forty. Seldom would they average less than one a fortnight. Many weeks contained several. She enjoyed them all, as she did everything; enjoyed meeting the people after the lecture, enjoyed inspecting the schools or towns where she spoke, enjoyed managing a demure country audience and conducting it decorously to a smile. Her subjects were generally taken from some phase of girls' education, occasionally from her experiences abroad or at home, or from a book she had been reading. I believe the majority of her addresses were unpaid, as were all the employments recorded in this chapter with the single exception of the Chicago deanship.

Such were some of the larger occupations of Mrs. Palmer's busy winters. The lesser ones I leave unnamed. Each autumn, in company with the Catholic priest, she engaged in that temperance campaign by which Cambridge has held unshaken for a long series of years its policy of No License. In each of the later Springs there were vacation schools to be organized and suitable play-grounds to be provided. Once a fortnight came the merry suppers of her sewing society, the ancient Cambridge "Bee." Each Friday Harvard students were met in Brooks House by Faculty wives; each Saturday in Boston the clever girls of the College Club expected her, their president for two years, at their afternoon tea. But every one knows how the occupations which devour time are either those petty matters which keep our humdrum world in motion, or else the erratic incalculable affairs which break into our regularities to-day and, because not likely to appear to-morrow, do for the moment claim exclusive attention. Of either we keep no chronicle. Yet a single serious one of the latter sort deserves mention. It fell on Mrs. Palmer in November, 1898, and cost her most of that winter. As she stepped from a street car opposite her door, a bicycle rider whirled round a neighboring corner and, before either could pause and with little fault on either side, struck her squarely, dashing her head against a paving stone. Complete consciousness did not return for twelve hours, and for a time permanent injury to the brain was feared. During the slow recovery she was much touched, and queerly surprised, by the expressions of sympathy which came to her from all parts of the country. Weakness remained for about a year, and her dark hair began to turn gray. But rest is medicinal, and Mrs. Palmer was not without the important ability to shirk. At the right moment she could sew, play, or take refuge in Boxford, leaving letters unanswered and committees unattended. Courage, a quiet mind, and a little nonchalance will heal much. By the time of her death all effects of the accident had passed away.

This account of Mrs. Palmer's busy winters may easily convey an erroneous impression. It is intended to be descriptive merely, not didactic. In it I have tried to depict Mrs. Palmer's working season, not to offer a program for persons in general. Let some women read the account with horror, rendered doubly thankful that they were born for the drawing room and easy chair. Let others be quickened in their own diverse professions and enter into them with the greater devotion because of Mrs. Palmer's labors. Let the plain housekeeper learn here how even under pressure one may keep cool, happy, and hardly in haste. Let each one draw from this story whatever moral it has for him or for her. With such uses of it I am not concerned. My business is simply to set forth a nature somewhat unusual, endowed with great powers whose exercise brought constant pleasure; endowed with a heart which could not be happy alone; with an originality that struck out its own ways of working and freshened every little act along its path; and with a piety that hourly hungered and thirsted after righteousness. In this season of what I have called her self-expression, delight and duty moved hand in hand. Each heavy-laden morning opened to her its opportunities and sent her forth gladly to meet its "good times." She would certainly never have wished others to follow in her track, but only to be earnest and joyous in their own. Laziness and conventionality she did indeed abhor, and thought most people only half awake. She liked to live in every fibre of her being, and so she vitalized all around. Yet her capacious life is only half reported in this chapter. As she conceived it, it was to hold both cares and carelessness. The prodigal winters of Cambridge were rendered possible by the supplemental peace of Boxford. To that contrasted spot let us now remove.

LETTERS

Is n't it strange that now in September, just after coming from abroad, I should be passing through Wellesley on the opening day of the College? There all must be turmoil and bustle, and ordinarily I should be going to the waiting work. Now I am flying to peaceful Boxford, with no wish to turn back to the old days. Yet as I speed along the familiar way, and my train at last dashes past the station, leaving the college towers in the distance, my feelings are too mixed to analyze. I only know that there is in them no touch of regret that the train does not leave me there. You are better than any college; to be your wife a higher position than the princess held in the days before you came and made her a queen.

This morning as I sat at work here at home Dr. F. threw open the door, led in an invalid girl whom he has been watching for several weeks, and said, "Lizzie is nineteen to-day, and I thought she would like to see the pretty things you brought from Europe." She has been holding the white lace dress in her lap all the afternoon. Her soft black eyes followed me about like Stella's, and her cough was sadly familiar. Her mother has just died of consumption, and she cannot live through the winter. When she went away, she put out her thin hands and said, "You have been very good to me. Won't you forget that you never saw me before, and let me kiss you?" Oh dear, how sad the world is! Why can't I put the white lace on her pretty form and send her out to find a lover like mine, and health and happiness with him?

I have missed you again. All day I have been presiding at the annual meeting of the Home Missionary Board in Park Street Church, the largest meeting the Association has ever held. At its close we contributed $800 to send another teacher to Dakota. I would gladly make an appointment for the morning; but I returned from New York late last night, and was at this meeting from nine until five o'clock to-day. A pile of letters demands immediate answers, and to-morrow at three o'clock the Executive Committee of Wellesley meets in Boston. Before or after that meeting I shall try to find you.

This is the first time I have been up long enough to write a note since Saturday. Last week I took a heavy cold, and perhaps I was tired. But I am all right now, or soon shall be. Your little card to-night brings tears to my eyes. I must see you. If I were n't afraid it would be better for you to have no one under your roof except your ownest ones, I should surely, surely, be with you at once. I believe I could smooth the aches out of your head and put you to sleep as if you were a little child. I know how, and love you enough to be able to do it. Won't you tell me something I may do for you? May I come some day and tell you a pretty story?

But no! As I write, I succumb. I shall go to-morrow. Tell your watchers and defenders that I won't speak, not a word! I'll only look; can't they trust me? Did they ever hear me talk much? Don't they know that I have n't any ideas left? Besides, I have a cold, and the doctor does n't allow me to say anything. I want to receive the pretty cushion you have made for me, stuffed with love and sewed with tenderness, from the very hands that made it. My head aches for it, and my heart — well, Longfellow said his was "hot and restless." Perhaps that is what I should say of mine if I were a poet. It is n't prudent for me to go out to-day — but to-morrow?

The time draws near for your speech. I am glad it comes on the first day of the festival, before you get tired. Then you will have it off your mind. Keep yourself fresh and calm until you have spoken, and then you can mingle with the people. What are you going to wear? You must tell me all about it when it is over, and you have had one good night's sleep.

As for the speech itself, it will make all the difference in the world how you say it. If you are heard distinctly, and your manner is cordial and earnest and unaffected, it will be a success. I would break up the first sentences a little. A speech is more effective if its early sentences are short. But this is a good one. I have thrown in a few quotations which I thought would be telling. Use them or not, as you please.

How in the world did you learn about Chicago? I trusted no whisper would reach you until I could speak. And I have been in bed for two weeks, am indeed just crawling about to-day. How I have longed for Florida or any haven of escape from Cambridge winds and dust! So I have planned little since President Harper was here three weeks ago. I have n't been willing to worry anybody in case we should not accept. But about this we ourselves don't know yet. We shall probably go to Chicago next week, during Harvard's Easter recess, look the ground over, and then decide as soon as possible. Of course I need n't say that we don't want to go. For almost every reason we prefer to stay just where we are. Undoubtedly it would be pleasanter and more useful to have $12,000 a year instead of four. And there are superb chances of work out there — how superb people here don't understand. What shall we do?

I am sorry to hear you speak sadly of your life and its small results, though what you say finds an echo in all our hearts when we stop to think of the gulf between our aspiration and accomplishment. The one comfort is that we do not know much about that accomplishment. I fancy you do not see your child grow from Sunday to Sunday. The child herself does n't know that she has grown at all. But with the Lord one day is as a thousand years, and a thousand years as one day. And indeed I wonder what more duties you could ask than those you are fulfilling so bravely. In the end I believe your town will be a better place because you live in it; and if so, all Maine and New England and our struggling world, that swings so slowly onward. Take heart, and let God bless all your life as wife and mother and daughter and friend and neighbor. You can't help being a strong influence quite unconsciously.

But consciously also you may help to think out help for many. Especially now as a mother, you can take thought for the children all about you and see that they have wholesome surroundings to grow in.

That is much on my mind of late. We comfortable women should do more than merely give to charities, hospitals, etc. We can keep the streets and schoolhouses clean and make half the diseases vanish. From our own blessed homes we can help to make the whole city a happy home for the little children who now hardly have homes at all. Why, what a fortunate woman you are! If I had a little daughter, it seems to me I should be proud to devote my whole time to her and her father and her home, and to sweetening her native town for her to live in.

But I am glad you are taking up music and are reading French and Dante. All this will keep a girl's heart in you, and an open mind, and make you fresher and gladder in your home. You will want your daughter to feel that you are a student too, when she becomes one, and that the learning is never done as long as we are in God's wonderful world. What a difference it will make when all our mothers have such relations with their children, besides the life of love!

We have been talking over your letter, and feel pretty certain that you ought not to give up your excellent place and devote yourself to your brother and his child. That would not be fair either to yourself or to him. He ought not to allow it. In the nature of things his plans must be very uncertain, while this is a critical period in your life. If just at your age you abandon your present opportunity for large influence and usefulness, withdrawing from scholarly work and surroundings, you will find after a few years that you cannot take it up anew. He in the mean time may marry again. He ought to be free to do so. But in that case you will be left without occupation or interest. I have seen this happen painfully often. No! Go on making your life as strong and valuable as you can. Have Nellie with you for a while and then put her into a good school. By and by that will be the very best thing for her. An only child needs school life earlier than other children.

Your present opportunity is an admirable one. Of course you must engage in it prudently, taking care of your health all the time. But when you are occupied with so beautiful a piece of work, your health is likely of itself to grow firmer. You seem to have been trusted as few women are; and that is "a call." It is a great thing to have won such confidence. It constitutes a capital. Into this work you can gather all your past experience and carry it straight on. You must not "shrink before the bigness of the task." That is what Wellesley has been trying to fit her daughters for, and you must not fail her when a chance for leadership comes. This is a remarkable offer, and in that very fact lies large promise of success. Of course no one can decide for you, especially if you feel no inner inclination. To me you seem well fitted. So many college women have no gift for executive work that those who have are the more necessary, if that important work is to be done.

I see you hesitate about abandoning your studies for a higher degree. Many young men and women are making a fetich of the Ph.D., letting splendid chances go by, as if that were an end in itself. It is a sad mistake, both for them and for society in general. Unless you have some definite scheme in mind, of long and patient research, you will not bring out results of consequence. Studying interesting questions among pleasant people is always agreeable, but it does n't make a life. My impression is that you are enough like me to prefer active work and direct influence to the solitary scholar's career. If I am right, you should not sacrifice a great opportunity for service, in case it appeals to you, for a little more lingering in lecture rooms and libraries.

A friend said to me the other day that women are already so occupied with the higher duties of life that they have no time to attend to political duties. She thought political duties would interfere with the proper execution of these higher ones, and rightly insisted that no such interference must be allowed. What then are the political duties? What are the higher duties? How far does the one kind obstruct or assist the other?

The political duties are informing one's self on the state of the country, on policies at issue, on candidates for office, and then going to the polls and depositing a ballot. The so-called higher duties are the bearing and rearing of children, while making a home for family and friends.

How much time must a woman spend on her political duties? If she belongs to the well-to-do class and hires others to do her domestic work, she has time for whatever interests her most — only let her interests be noble! If she does her own housework, she can take ten minutes to stop on her way to market for voting once or twice a year. She can find half an hour a day for newspapers and other means of information. She can talk with her family and friends about what she reads. This she does now; she will then do it more intelligently and will give and receive more from what she says and hears.

The duties of motherhood and the making of a home are the most sacred work for women of every class, and the dearest to them. If casting an intelligent vote would interfere with what woman alone can do — and what, if failed in, undermines society and government — no one can question which a woman should choose. But it cannot be shown that there is any large number of women in this country who have not the necessary time to vote intelligently. Study of the vital questions of our government would make them better comrades to their husbands and friends, better guides to their sons, and more interesting and valuable members of society. Women have more leisure than men; they are less tied to hours of routine; they usually have more years of school training, and in this country their conscience and loyalty compare favorably with men's. All this makes simple the combination of public and "higher" duties.

The objections to the political woman and to the educated woman present some instructive analogies. Fifty years ago it was seriously believed that knowing the classics would ruin a girl's morals, knowing philosophy her religion, and mathematics her health; in general, a college education would take away her desire to be a good wife and mother. To protect a being so frail the colleges were carefully closed against her. Now, with the approval of wise men, more girls than boys are preparing for college, and this in the public interest. It may be found in politics, as in education, that the higher duties of women will be assisted, not hindered, by intelligent discipline in the lower.

The report on the Endowment of Fellowships is admirably drawn. Whether the decision is for

European or American advanced study, I shall support it as far as I am able, and I believe the necessary money can easily be obtained. Yet I hope the Association will decide on European study. Our committee keeps us properly protected against every danger to our students except the family; but that is serious. A young woman cannot hold herself apart from a needy family, as a young man can. And while many a young woman can get advantages in certain lines of study pursued in America as well as abroad, still on the whole and in the present development of women's scholarship, I believe the Association will accomplish more and be more secure of its results if it sends its Fellow abroad into an entirely new field. There a sick brother cannot claim her for a month's nursing, nor a lonely mother be likely to demand to be amused. No! Foreign life has not made me exactly inhuman, but we need to strengthen women to devote themselves to high, persistent work; and there is too little proper sentiment in America about the sacredness of their time, as we all know.

In this distant city the women's Civic Club has good material but bad leadership. The meeting last night was in the Presbyterian Church, and more than a dozen former Wellesley girls were present. There were four addresses before mine; so I spoke about twenty minutes, and am afraid I was too critical to suit the mass of the audience. In fact I was burning with indignation over the president, Mrs. T. She is a ranting sentimentalist, a Methodist of the worst type. I cannot understand how this woman has done what she really has done. A description of her talk cannot be put on paper. But more hopeless conceit and vulgarity, more cheap sentimentality I have never known packed into a single hour. At the close of my address she threw her arms around me, called me "my darling," and begged me to bring my trunk at once to her house. Many in the audience wiped their eyes with delight at her way of saying "Jesus," and looked disgusted at my lack of "spirituality." These women will have to learn that sprinkling rose-water does not cure the cancers of city life. But don't suppose I said anything so heretical here.

Last week I was fortunate enough to have a talk with a Cape Cod farmer at a little railroad station where our train was delayed. As we grew confidential he told me how, though he was not yet sixty years old, he had seen all the dreams of his boyhood come true. This surprised me into asking him to be more confidential still and to tell me what they were. He did so in detail. There was the mortgage on the farm when he was a boy, and the heavy load when he inherited the farm. He said, "I should have been swamped by it if I had n't had the luck just then to fall in love with the nicest girl on the Cape. And I don't mind telling you," he went on, "what I told her. I told her that if she would join me I would work hard, and we would scrimp and save and pay off that mortgage. I told her too that before I got into my grave I would earn enough and lay by enough so that every one of my women-folks should sit in a rocking-chair reading a story every afternoon of their lives." I thanked my farmer then, and I bless him still. His story is an American classic. It tells the dream of all the chivalrous husbands and fathers and brothers and sons of our American women — a glorious dream, if the women refuse the rocking-chair and the story; but a pitiful one if they take these every afternoon of their lives. Never in all the world has so much leisure, so much money, or so much freedom in the spending of both, been granted women as to us to-day. But how slenderly we are fitted for using that money and leisure nobly!

This morning I am asked to write something about Miss A. and send it by the next mail to the Magazine. How difficult it is to fit such things to the intricate reality, and so how untruthful they generally are! When I suddenly leave you all, I hope nobody will have to say anything about me, or plan a "Memorial Number." Love and silence are best.

You will find some hardship in this change, but don't take it harder than you need. Comfort yourself, as I often do, with the thought that rest comes sure and soon. Neither you nor I are any longer young, and we both come of a short-lived race. After all, it makes little difference what happens, or when.

XIII

BOXFORD

ABOUT twenty-five miles to the north of Boston, and half a dozen inland from the sea, lies the ancient village of Boxford, settled among its trees. These hem the sight on every side. Wherever you go in this rolling country, you seldom leave the woods; and even in crossing its two considerable plains, jagged peaks of pines form always the sawlike sky-line. Encircled by these woods lie many ponds, and the streams which run to and fro are met with bewildering frequency. On them is an occasional saw-mill, where piles of sawdust perfume the air. So important are our streams that we carefully distinguish their varieties. West of New York everything that runs is a "creek." Brook, as a spoken word, is gone—the most regrettable loss the English language has suffered in America. With us a creek does not run, but is a crack or inlet of the sea. Our largest current is Topsfield River; in the second grade of things that flow we put our many brooks; and that which runs swiftly a part of the year, and shows a dry bed for the remainder we fittingly call a run. I do not know if the word occurs elsewhere between us and Bull Run.

In speaking of Boxford it is more natural to tell first of its woods, ponds, and brooks than of its houses and people, because there are so many more of them. The town is nine miles long by five wide, but there are more half miles without a house than with one. The village itself contains only a dozen, beside the single church, the single store, the small public library, and the large town hall. Driving along the stone-walled roads, one comes at intervals on solitary farmsteads where a venerable house and large barn sit in smooth fields, sharply sundered from the forest. The older houses sit square to the compass, regardless of the road. Everything about them is in order, as was ordained two hundred years ago; paint, thrift, and self-respect having maintained the standard since. The soil is thin, and the returns from farming meagre. Formerly summer crops of hay, oats, and wheat were profitable; and in the little shoe-shops, which still stand deserted beside many houses, the farmer and his children kept busy through the winter. But Boxford has been unable to hold its own against the farming of the West or the machinery of Lynn and Brockton. The young men — and of later years, since more avenues of employment have been opened, the young women too — leave the town as soon as possible. Our population, less than it was a century ago, barely reaches five hundred. Almost entirely it is of English stock, the same families continuing on their lands through many generations. Hardly any Italians, Canadians, or Irish are here. There are no poor, no rich; nor have we any doctor or lawyer. There are too few people to quarrel; and in our wholesome piney air dying and falling sick went out of fashion ages ago.

This is the village which in Mrs. Palmer's affections possessed a sacredness no other spot of earth could claim. Into it had soaked the traditions of my family for eight generations. To it her own early nature-worship had been transferred and here became newly enriched by many hallowed experiences. Here was her refuge when elsewhere the world was too much with her. The hush and peace of Boxford she has herself expressed in compact verse: —

Out of the roar and din,
  Safely shut in,
Out of the seething street,
  Silence to meet.

Out of the hurrying hours,
  To lie in flowers;
Far from the toil and strife
  To find our life.

Ah, let the world forget!
  Here we have met.
Most in this sacred place
  I see thy face.

Our farm in Boxford has never been owned by anybody but ourselves and the Indians. Captain John Peabody built his house here in 1660, and out of it came that tribe of Peabodys who have since wandered into every state of the Union and even made their name blest in far-away London. Until 1856 the farm continued in that single name. Then by the death of my grandfather it descended to my mother, Lucy Peabody, and has for the last fifty years been known as the Palmer farm. Of its hundred and twenty-five acres about half is woodland. Its large two-chimneyed house stands in an open field or park of twenty acres, dotted with trees which mark the line of the run and enclose a small sheet of water. Oaks and maples fill the rocky pasture in the rear; while across the road, and at about an equal distance in front, the sandier soil is covered with pines. Perhaps the feature of this bit of ground which was most loved by Mrs. Palmer is the twenty-foot brook, which, after sauntering through the tall pines, zigzags through meadows and yields us, in addition to its beauty and murmur, the more solid delights of pickerel, lilies, stepping-stones, and bathing-pool.

In the woods for about two miles run paths, or avenues rather, cut in large part by Mrs. Palmer and myself, each enriched by special associations and suitably endowed by her with names. Names too have gathered about other prominent features of the farm. The Fairy Ring is an open circle in the woods; the Old Cellar, a hollow ringed with cedars, still shows the foundations of a house which was already gone in 1800; at Sunset Rock on Sunday afternoons nearly all Shakespeare's plays have been read aloud; and Hattie's House, a rock among the ash trees, where one may recline, was the favorite haunt of an invalid member of the household, long since dead. No part of this farm is mere earth and vegetation. Clustering associations cover the soil. All entered long ago into that alliance with man which in Lord Bacon's judgment is ever a condition of beauty,— *homo additus naturae*. Raw nature is pretty poor stuff. Most philosophers doubt if, parted from man, matter would be quite conceivable. Coleridge thought that in beholding the world —

> We receive but what we give,
> And in our life alone does nature live.

At any rate, human emotions intertwined with nature ennoble both material objects and themselves. Things loved cease to be mere things, and retain longer than rose-jars a delicate perfume. So did the glorifying magic of affection permeate Boxford. Mrs. Palmer found the place deeply impregnated by the eventful past. When she died, she had given it the impress of her pervasive personality.

Her home was not the old house of the first settler.

This fell into decay in my childhood. Nor was it even the stately second house, built on the original farm in 1825 by my grandfather. During Mrs. Palmer's life this was occupied by my sister and half a dozen others who might by an affectionate arithmetic be counted members of the family. Her home was on an adjoining lot, a stone's throw distant but unparted by boundaries. It is a small, picturesque structure, with central chimney, and is almost hidden by foliage. It sits on its little bank like a turtle on a log. Half a century ago it came into my family, but was then already a hundred and fifty years old. In its low rooms, each having a big fire-place, one easily touches the ceilings with the hand. Across the ceiling of the large living room runs the supporting oak beam. The chamber above is wainscoted with pine which time has deepened almost to mahogany. Shutters of the same wood slide across its windows.

But the outside of this house is more important than the inside, though between the two there is little distinction; for the floor is on a level with the ground, and long diamond windows give exit on all sides, while porch and large bay-window bind it still more closely to the earth. East and west are piazzas, so sheltered with shrubbery as to increase the nest-like aspect, the western being fitted as an outdoor study and shielded from every storm. Tables and chairs and bookshelves and sofa are on it, and in the

BOXFORD HOUSE

rear it connects with a library of fifteen hundred volumes. On it we live and work. When people talk of the necessity of exercise they chiefly mean the necessity of breathing open air. In such an outdoor workshop as I have described it is easy to give half a dozen hours a day to books and writing; then with a couple of hours in the woods toward evening, and a bath in the brook on the way home, one comes out at the end of the summer in vigorous health.

Such was Mrs. Palmer's happy hiding-place. No telegraph connects it with the city, the station is a mile from the village, our house half a mile from this, the railroad a branch line, and there is no hotel. Here she was fairly secure from invasion. There were no calls to make, no lectures to give, no committees to meet, and little company was invited. Occasionally the daughter of a friend was with us, and of the congenial company in the ancestral house we saw as little or as much as we liked. "Winters for other people," we used to say, "summers for ourselves." It took some time, however, to break up brazen habits of incessant work; and in the early years Mrs. Palmer was often doubtful about duty. "Do you think we have a right to such happiness?" she would ask. But soon discovering how she accumulated here the stock of energy, learning, and romance from which the world drew so copiously during the busy season, she reconciled herself to her bliss and accepted the peace and companionship in which her soul delighted. People who found her lamp a light to their feet on city streets did not know the Boxford fields in which its oil was grown. But there is no feature of joy more creditable than its inevitably communicative character. He who is filled with happiness, though seemingly absorbed, emanates pleasure on whoever crosses his way. He cannot contain it all, but produces much for his neighbors. There is no other such agent for diffusing joy as the heart that itself enjoys. This Mrs. Palmer possessed by nature. In Boxford the springs of her effluent gladness were newly filled.

Long before our marriage her restful associations with Boxford began. Early in our acquaintance, and twice afterwards, she visited me here in company with a friend. The summer of 1887, after our engagement was announced, she spent in my old house with her sister, while I lived with our farmer. Here we came for the fortnight after our wedding, when the pine boughs were loaded with snow and the world without and within was like fairyland. Here in subsequent years we often returned to celebrate that anniversary, or — more beautiful still — for the early spring recess. Scattered up and down the working time many Sundays found us here, apple-blossom Sunday never failing. Though May and June were too hurried a season to be passed here in full, we usually contrived a few days then for observing nature's miracles. And never does nature appear more miraculous than to the tired eyes of the dweller in cities when, after absence, he once more rests them on green fields stretched out against dark trees. I suspect Milton had for a while been a stranger at Horton when he wrote "L'Allegro." Among Mrs. Palmer's papers I find a kindred outburst of astonished country joy: —

We journeyed through sweet woodland ways,
My Love and I.
The maples set the shining fields ablaze.
The blue May sky
Brought to us its great Spring surprise;
While we saw all things through each other's eyes.

And sometimes from a steep hillside
Shone fair and bright
The shadbush, like a young June bride,
Fresh clothed in white.
Sometimes came glimpses glad of the blue sea;
But I smiled only on my Love. He smiled on me.

The violets made a field one mass of blue,
Even bluer than the sky;
The little brook took on that color too,
And sang more merrily.

"Your dress is blue," he laughing said. "Your eyes,"
My heart sang, "sweeter than the bending skies."

We spoke of poets dead so long ago,
And their wise words.
We glanced at apple trees, like drifted snow;
We watched the nesting birds, —
Only a moment! Ah, how short the day!
Yet all the winters cannot blow its sweetness quite away.

What were Mrs. Palmer's occupations in this idyllic spot? Letters largely; for even when all other human ties are cut, these tentacles search out the runaway and seize him where he hides. But two hours generally sufficed to clear Mrs. Palmer's day of their clutches. Then birds and books, cooking and sewing were at hand. Having a pretty extensive knowledge of birds, which I with my short sight was denied, she tried to spend a little time each day sitting about the fields, in attendance on her wayward friends. When she was working in the house and I on the piazza, I was charged to catch each novel sound or sight and speak it not too loudly, so that she might glide forth with the opera glass. I find memoranda of one hundred and forty varieties of birds discovered on the farm. She loved them all; not the rare ones only, but those which make the ordinary pleasure of the day. Bobolinks, cuckoos, and whip-poor-wills abound in spring; wood-thrushes, her favorites among all birds, in the summer. Vireos and orioles are in pretty constant song. Owls laugh and hoot at night. Among the thick foliage flash tanagers, jays, blue-birds, yellow-birds. Humming-birds come every ten minutes to the tiger lilies by the piazza, and on one of its rafters each spring a phœbe builds and brings out her three broods. In and out of a hollow tree by our window flickers were always moving, and into the nest of a song-sparrow we looked as we raised our curtain. She loved the clear call of the quail and the drum of the partridge. On the whole, she cared more for birds than for the abundant and lovely wild flowers. They were more alive. Yet most of the flowers she knew, and had them always on her tables. It made a kind of festival when I brought her the first columbine, the first wild rose, the first cardinal, or the first blue gentian. The boisterous golden-rod and the wide variety of opulent asters told her that the year had turned, and touched her with a sort of harvest sadness. The pale stalks of the early meadow rue pleased her better. But she had a heart fitted also for clover and apple blossoms, for buttercups and dandelions, and whatever common brightness spots the fertile earth. And then there were the butterflies, the bees in the linden, the squirrels, the woodchucks, the foxes. The behavior of all these pretty creatures of the country engaged her as closely as the winter perplexities of girls.

There was pleasure too in catching at the right moment the successive crops of berries and fruits, and preserving them or turning them into jellies. She acquired some renown for skill in persuading jellies to stiffen. Her rows of glasses she contemplated as a miser his money-bags, knowing their power of carrying summer sweetness to winter tables. Those made elsewhere were thought to lack the full Boxford flavor. Other experiments in cookery could be tried here, and the Boxford table must always have a special delicacy and neatness. If I missed her in the library, I was pretty sure to find her in the kitchen. But all the housekeeping was kept simple. Our home, convenient and beautiful enough, was of the earlier type, plain and with its pleasures rooted in elemental things. The modern city establishment, incongruously dropped among fields where it never grew, yields no such easy conjunction with nature.

In later years she turned to photography; and as soon as a new section of pathway in the woods was accomplished, it was transferred to paper and taken to Cambridge for her winter desk. She experimented with different methods of developing and printing; and I must fit up a dark closet with appropriate pans, acids, and waters. But in two respects her education had been defective. The busy years had allowed her no practice in music; and though she could pick out a strain on the piano, for solid enjoyment she was dependent on the performance of others. For similar reasons she knew no games until after she left Wellesley, and summers were too short for acquiring many. In two or three, however, she became proficient. There was a species of solitaire which she liked, though she soon adjusted it so as to enable two persons to work together toward a common end. She remade casino so that two players could waste a half-hour over it without regret. Dominoes was her favorite when three could play. Its luck was largely reduced by the division of all pieces at the start, by the exclusion of a pool, and the mechanical turning up of the twenty-eighth piece. Devices were found for keeping the hands decently clear of doublets, and skill was set free to operate the long suits, to reckon what pieces were in an opponent's hand, to get control of an end, or to block the game while leaving few spots in the hand of the blockader. A domino score was kept through the summer, or even from year to year; and on the piazza most days after dinner three opponents struggled to shift that score in rival directions. In whist she never became expert. Too seldom were four present in playtime. And chess she did not learn, as too much like winter labors. But though she was unfortunately past thirty when she first took up technical games, she found herself not unprepared. Everything had been a game for her. Throughout life she had been watching contrivance and circumstance as they run side by side, and had delighted in the contest by which the worse is brought into subjection to the better.

At Boxford too one could sew; and in sewing she delighted, as Izaak Walton in fishing. It was a contemplative occupation and an excuse for peace, one of the superiorities of her sex. As the needle pushed its way along the seam, there came leisure for dreaming, remembering, planning. She resorted to it often when alone; and as I read aloud, she would hem napkins and table-cloths as peacefully as a cat purrs. Usually there was mending at hand, and embroidery could be taken at a pinch. But the more aggressive forms of sewing were the favorites. From time to time I would miss her for a day at her desk. She had disappeared into untraceable upper regions. When she presented herself at night, I must admire the old gown reconstructed, or the spring hat which had become an autumn one. Over these triumphs she rejoiced as I at completing a magazine article. But such happy toils were not allowed to invade our evenings. These were reserved for books and early bed hours.

Of course books were the commonest employment for both of us. I had my urgent studies, and close at hand she hers. In winter time it was impossible to amass much scholarly capital. Broken up as we were by engagements and lectures, study then could merely respond to immediate needs. But in the uninterrupted hours of the blessed summer one could explore and heap up knowledge. Not that she even then undertook severe connected studies; I certainly discouraged them. Her summer was for rest. And then too she was not a bookish person, but primarily a woman of affairs who fed herself best by direct observation of men and things. Yet from books she derived great stimulus and was always longing to come at them more closely. Her actual dealings with them were peculiar. They were entirely subordinated to her life and never acquired rights of their own. Sometimes she would go a month without opening one; then at a moment of unexpected leisure she would seize whatever came to hand — story, verse, abstract discussion, it made little difference how severe the subject — and instantly she was absorbed. Nothing could shake her attention. Questions went unanswered, and even letters neglected. She read with intensity and speed. I have rarely known her to take more than half a day for any volume, however substantial, and afterwards she knew whatever her book contained. Naturally during the summer these times of burial in a book were more permissible, and she revelled in the opportunity.

Long before we married both she and I were devotees of English poetry; of that poetry, I mean, in its historic relations and not merely in its single authors. She brought from Wellesley a good acquaintance with both the earlier and the later material, and increased it through every year we were together. The seventeenth-century poets were especially dear, though of course the enormous and passionately ethical product of the nineteenth was still oftener in our hands. I am inclined to think that all profitable communion with poetry has in it an element of stealth. It cannot be arranged for, like other interests; but requiring more of personal response than they, can reach its best results only when stolen from moments already more or less pledged. I at least have formed my deepest intimacies with the poets when I have come upon them by way of interruption. During the busy winter, whenever Mrs. Palmer and I grew tired, work was cast aside and we would snatch an evening for the restful singers. I would read aloud, while she sewed or gazed at the fire. There is no such means for clearing cobwebs from a weary brain as sweeping it with disinfectant rhythms. Better than music it is for me because, while it is no less sportive than music, its play is ever with rationalities. By such interruptions, then, we kept ourselves in the best condition both for poetry and daily work.

Now Boxford was one long interruption, contrived for play, beauty, and idealism. Out of that soil poetry grew as naturally as grass in the field. It was read because it was lived. As we roamed the woods we talked it, discussing the methods and psychology of the writers we had been reading. A book of verses was often with us underneath the bough. And when the nights were fair we would carry a shaded light into the pines, and gathering a considerable company from the two houses, all as mad as we, would lie on the fragrant needles and read an evening through. I remember one August night having the entire "Midsummer Night's Dream" in the Fairy Ring, when owls became our chorus, and the moon sifted through the branches as if it were Bottom's lantern. Naturally then when, moved by her own experience of a kind of Golden Age, she began, as I have related in my first chapter, to write verse herself, her lines on love, nature, and God — themes never parted in her mind — had an easy depth and veracity seldom met in the tangled and groping poetry of our time. A few examples of her country verse I print.

It is pleasant to write this lyric chapter on her Boxford home, because previously I have so often been obliged to exhibit her under harsh conditions. She had always a heart most easily made glad, but her stern early years gave slender opportunity for indulging its capacity for delight. In Boxford this was legitimately let loose. Needing little outward stimulus because of inward peace, it fastened on the small occasions of the country and drew from them gaiety and health. Here we went out with joy and were led forth with peace. Mountains and hills broke forth before us into singing, and all the trees of the fields clapped their hands. Not that troubles did not sometimes overleap our hedges; we had our share. Death did not pass us by, nor illness either. Our projects did not always succeed. In a few instances, saddest of all, the characters of those we loved collapsed. But guarded as we were by each other, such things did not crush or appall. What would terrify another usually left Mrs. Palmer undisturbed. One day as she lay ill, a thunder storm came swiftly out of the southwest and struck the house, destroying the room adjoining her own. She seemed at the time much interested in the novel event, as if it were something contrived for her entertainment. Only after her death I found among her papers a hymn with that date attached. It was sung at the Memorial Service held in Harvard College Chapel. I print it here under the title of "The Tempest."

LETTERS

We are finding Boxford the same restful spot as always, only at this Easter season more peaceful still. The refreshment of it fills heart and brain. You know how country hours dream themselves away. We seem to have been here but a day, and on Wednesday must go reluctantly back to Cambridge. The skies have been delicious — warm sun, with fresh west wind, and melting moonlight among the pines at night. The fields are greening, and our one day of gentle constant rain is bringing the wild flowers through the dead leaves. There are none in actual blossom yet. But the robins are making themselves at home in the fields and apple trees, and the swallows and bluebirds are important over spring house-hunting and settling. I know how they feel.

It is a glowing spring morning. The transformation of the world is wonderful. Everything you see is a surprise. The fields have that vivid green which is so brief. The crops stand in shining rows two inches high. The streams are full of sparkling water, the maples flaming red, willows in their spring glory, and all the light woods a-flutter with young leaves. They plainly hint of bloodroot and hepatica. Everywhere spring work goes on: plowing in some places, sowing and planting in others, gardening and housecleaning wherever people live. Yesterday we went through the wood paths, clearing away the winter's droppings. That's what we came for — the silence of the pine woods. Such infinite stillness gives me a kind of awe. And to-morrow we must be at our desks in Cambridge!

Our servant is enchanted with Boxford, begging me to remain here all the year, wishing the old house were in Cambridge, "if we must live there." This delights me and assures a peaceful kitchen for the summer. She has been helping me plant seeds about the windows — morning-glories, sweet peas, pansies, nasturtiums. We have upholstered several chairs and painted others, setting our house in order. G. is wonderfully well. He is working on his Homer, which comes out this summer and keeps him steadily busy.

So this is blessed Boxford again! We saw it at five o'clock to-day, and are already adjusting ourselves to it with expansive satisfaction. Did we ever find it so green and sweet before? The haying is just begun, and the fields are superb, with the grass up to my waist, all full of clover and daisies and buttercups. Wild roses are in blossom by the Run. The phœbe is raising her second brood on the piazza, and in the old apple trees the young robins and bluebirds are learning to fly. You should be here to help me see their awkward ways. As I write in the library a whip-poor-will comes into the ash tree and sings as if he were in the room itself, an owl calls far away in the pines, and the moonlight on the Park turns it into fairy land.

We were amazed at the coolness and freshness of this refuge yesterday, when after the fierce heat of Cambridge we again found ourselves under our vines. It is a delicious world, the second "sea-turn" within a week softening and refreshing all. I wish I could send some of it to you, send too some of my easy housekeeping. In this respect Boxford improves. This year we have more provision-wagons coming to our door. Twice a week a man brings us fish straight from the sea. Ask H. if she will have steamed Duxbury clams or a broiled live lobster for lunch. I wish you might see how attractive the old rooms look with their new curtains, green and white, and the new coverings for the lounges and window seats. And then we have time here, we two. Last night by lamplight we sat late on the piazza, while G. read aloud a French novel. And there he sits now, swaying back and forth as he reads or watches the haymakers in the Park, or pats the dog at his feet, who hardly turns his head from gazing far away at the woodchucks in the field. It does my heart good to be in such scenes. Here is quiet for tired nerves that makes one able to meet anything smilingly afterwards.

We shall expect you on Saturday afternoon. Dear me! I wish the house were not so little. Two rooms are hardly large enough for seven Wellesley girls. But my heart is large enough, and I want them all for Sunday. That will give time for at least seven good talks. And what a glorious set of girls it is, as you name them over, every one of them! This week the cook has been on a vacation, though she will be here when you arrive. But you should have tasted the nice things I have cooked. G. says my bread is the very best he has ever eaten, and my currant jelly and preserves are beautiful to behold. How you will enjoy the fragrant haying and the cardinal flowers in the Run!

THE TEMPEST

He shall give His angels charge
  Over thee in all thy ways.
Though the thunders roam at large,
  Though the lightning round me plays,
Like a child I lay my head
In sweet sleep upon my bed.

Though the terror come so close,
  It shall have no power to smite;
It shall deepen my repose,
  Turn the darkness into light.

Touch of angels' hands is sweet;
Not a stone shall hurt my feet.

All Thy waves and billows go
  Over me to press me down
Into arms so strong I know
  They will never let me drown.
Ah, my God, how good Thy will!
I will nestle and be still.

HALLOWED PLACES

I pass my days among the quiet places
  Made sacred by your feet.
The air is cool in the fresh woodland spaces,
  The meadows very sweet.

The sunset fills the wide sky with its splendor,
  The glad birds greet the night.
I stop and listen for a voice strong, tender,
  I wait those dear eyes' light.

You are the heart of every gleam of glory,
  Your presence fills the air;
About you gathers all the fair year's story,
  I read you everywhere.

BEFORE THE MOWING

Never a sunny morning
Fuller of bliss.
Never gladder faces
Felt the sun's warm kiss
Than my meadow blossoms,
Dreaming not of this.

Wild roses beckoned
All along the Run;
Hardhack and meadow rue
Sang, "The night is done!"
All the grasses waved their hands
And welcomed back the sun.

Daisies and clovers
Nestled side by side;
Buttercups and black-eyed Susans
Tossed their heads in pride;
And a tall field lily
Looked at me and sighed.

Ah, my meadow grasses,
How your breath is sweet!
How you shelter happy homes
Safe around your feet!
How you shine, relentless death
Suddenly to meet!

SUMMER RAIN

Stand with me here,
My very dear!
Watch the swift armies of the summer rain
Sweep the tall grasses of the Park,
Changing our shining noonday into dark.
Hear the loud thunder roar, again, again,
And roll and triumph in this summer rain.

The little birds all hide;
The cattle, wandering wide,
Seek the safe shelter of a spreading tree;
The old dog crouches by his master's feet.
Dark clouds come on, an army, strong and fleet.
Crash follows crash, all things to covert flee;
And wind and lightning drive me, — close to thee!

THE BUTTERFLY

I hold you at last in my hand,
Exquisite child of the air.
Can I ever understand
How you grew to be so fair?

You came to my linden tree
To taste its delicious sweet,

I sitting here in the shadow and shine
Playing around its feet.

Now I hold you fast in my hand,
You marvelous butterfly,
Till you help me to understand
The eternal mystery.

From that creeping thing in the dust
To this shining bliss in the blue!
God give me courage to trust
I can break my chrysalis too!

NIGHTFALL

The dear, long, quiet summer day
Draws to its close.
To the deep woods I steal away
To hear what the sweet thrush will say
In her repose.

Beside the brook the meadow rue
Stands tall and white.
The water softly slips along,
A murmur to the thrush's song
To greet the night.

Over and over, like a bell,
Her song rings clear;
The trees stand still in joy and prayer.
Only the angels stir the air,
High Heaven bends near.

I bow my head and lift my heart
In thy great peace.
Thy Angelus, my God, I heed.
By the still waters wilt thou lead
Till days shall cease.

ON A GLOOMY EASTER

I hear the robins singing in the rain.
The longed-for Spring is hushed so drearily
That hungry lips cry often wearily,
"Oh, if the blessed sun would shine again!"

I hear the robins singing in the rain.
The misty world lies waiting for the dawn,
The wind sobs at my window and is gone,
And in the silence come old throbs of pain.

But still the robins sing on in the rain;
Not waiting for the morning sun to break,
Nor listening for the violets to wake,
Nor fearing lest the snow may fall again.

My heart sings with the robins in the rain;
  For I remember it is Easter morn,
And life and love and peace are all newborn,
  And joy has triumphed over loss and pain.

Sing on, brave robins, sing on in the rain!
  You know behind the clouds the sun must shine;
You know that death means only life divine,
  And all our losses turn to heavenly gain.

I lie and listen to you in the rain.
  Better than Easter bells that do not cease,
Your message from the heart of God's great peace.
  And to his arms I turn and sleep again.

DECEMBER

Only half a year ago, Love,
  Did we pass this way?
Now the ground is white with snowdrifts,
  Chill the clouds and gray.

Then the river wandered softly
  Onward to the sea;
All the glad world sang in chorus
  Just for you and me.

Full of light and sound and fragrance,
Night shone more than day;
Till we held our breath in rapture,
And in silence lay.

Now the earth is cold and lifeless,
All the trees are bare;
Only now and then a snowflake
Wanders through the air.

But your hand sweeps all my heartstrings
To a joyful tune;
In the world it may be winter,
In my life 't is June.

So in meeting or in parting,
Winter time or Spring,
You still fill my life with beauty,
Teach my days to sing.

A COMMUNION HYMN

How sweet and silent is the place,
My God, alone with thee!
Awaiting here thy touch of grace,
Thy heavenly mystery.

So many ways thou hast, dear Lord,
My longing heart to fill:
Thy lovely world, thy spoken word,
The doing thy sweet will,

Giving thy children living bread,
Leading thy weak ones on,
The touch of dear hands on my head,
The thought of loved ones gone.

Lead me by many paths, dear Lord,
But always in thy way;
And let me make my earth a Heaven
Till next Communion Day.

While I was in Boston [writes Gertrude W. Fielder] I had the pleasure of meeting Alice Freeman Palmer. She was a doer of the word, and not a hearer only; for almost every week through the hot summer she used to leave her peaceful, calm retreat in the country and go to Boston to talk to children of the slums at a vacation school. These schools are kept up through the summer in the poorest localities. The children are given a morning's session of music, reading, and pretty water-color sketches, to look at. They can bring the babies with them; and many indeed could not come at all without the little ones. Here is the story as Mrs. Palmer told it: —

One July morning I took an early train. It was a day that gave promise of being very, very hot even in the country, and what in the city! When I reached my destination I found a great many girls in the room, but more babies than girls, it seemed. Each girl was holding one, and there were a few to spare. "Now," I said, "what shall I talk to you about this morning, girls?" "Talk about life," said one girl. Imagine! "I am afraid that is too big a subject for such a short time," I said.

Then up spoke a small, pale-faced, heavy-eyed child, with a great fat baby on her knee, "Tell us how to be happy." The tears rushed to my eyes, and a lump came in my throat. Happy in such surroundings as those in which, no doubt, she lived: perhaps dirty and foul-smelling! Happy, with burdens too heavy to be borne! All this flashed through my mind while the rest took up the word and echoed, "Yes, tell us how to be happy."

"Well," I said, "I will give you my three rules for being happy; but mind, you must all promise to keep them for a week, and not skip a single day, for they won't work if you skip one single day." So they all faithfully and solemnly promised that they would n't skip a single day.

"The first rule is that you will commit something to memory every day, something good. It need n't be much, three or four words will do, just a pretty bit of a poem, or a Bible verse. Do you understand?" I was so afraid they would n't, but one little girl with flashing black eyes jumped up from the corner of the room and cried, "I know; you want us to learn something we 'd be glad enough to remember if we went blind." "That 's it, exactly!" I said. "Something you would like to remember if you went blind." And they all promised that they would, and not skip a single day.

"The second rule is: Look for something pretty every day; and don't skip a day, or it won't work. A leaf, a flower, a cloud — you can all find something. Is n't there a park somewhere near here that you can all walk to?" (Yes, there was one.) "And stop long enough before the pretty thing that you have spied to say, 'Is n't it beautiful!' Drink in every detail, and see the loveliness all through. Can you do it?" They promised, to a girl.

"My third rule is — now, mind, don't skip a day — Do something for somebody every day." "Oh, that 's easy!" they said, though I thought it would be the hardest thing of all. Just think, that is what those children said, "Oh, that 's easy! Did n't they have to tend babies and run errands every day, and was n't that doing something for somebody?" "Yes," I answered them, "it was."

At the end of the week, the day being hotter than the last, if possible, I was wending my way along a very narrow street, when suddenly I was literally grabbed by the arm, and a little voice said, "I done it!" "Did what!" I exclaimed, looking down, and seeing at my side a tiny girl with the proverbial fat baby asleep in her arms. Now I will admit that it was awfully stupid of me not to know, but my thoughts were far away, and I actually did not know what she was talking about. "What you told us to, and I never skipped a day, neither," replied the child, in a rather hurt tone. "Oh," I said, "now I know what you mean. Put down the baby, and let's talk about it." So down on the sidewalk she deposited the sleeping infant, and she and I stood over it and talked.

"Well," she said, "I never skipped a day, but it was awful hard. It was all right when I could go to the park, but one day it rained and rained, and the baby had a cold, and I just could n't go out, and I thought sure I was going to skip, and I was standin' at the window, 'most cryin', and I saw" — here her little face brightened up with a radiant smile — "I saw a sparrow takin' a bath in the gutter that goes round the top of the house, and he had on a black necktie, and he was handsome." It was the first time I had heard an English sparrow called handsome, but I tell you it was n't laughable a bit — no, not a bit.

"And then, there was another day," she went on, "and I thought I should have to skip it, sure. There was n't another thing to look at in the house. The baby was sick, and I could n't go out, and I was feelin' terrible, when" — here she caught me by both hands, and the most radiant look came to her face — "I saw the baby's hair!" "Saw the baby's hair!" I echoed. "Yes, a little bit of sun came in the window, and I saw his hair, an' I'll never be lonesome any more." And catching up the baby from the sidewalk, she said, "See!" and I too saw the baby's hair. "Is n't it beau-ti-ful?" she asked. "Yes, it is beautiful," I answered. You have heard of artists raving over Titian hair. Well, as the sun played on this baby's hair, there were the browns, the reds, the golds, which make up the Titian hair. Yes, it was truly beautiful. "Now, shall we go on?" I said, taking the heavy baby from her.

The room was literally packed this time; ten times as many girls, and as many babies as your mind will conceive of. I wish you could have listened with me to the experiences of those little ones. Laughter and tears were so commingled that I don't know which had the mastery.

XIV

DEATH

"We make too much of the circumstance men call death. All life is one. All service one, be it here or there. Death is only a little door from one room to another. We had better not think much about it, nor be afraid for ourselves or for those who are dear to us; but rather make life here so rich and sweet and noble that this will be our Heaven. We need no other till He comes and calls us to larger life and fresh opportunity."

So spoke Mrs. Palmer at the funeral of a friend, and such was always her habit, — to make little account of death. In accordance with her wise words I should naturally record here only the bare fact that she died in Paris on December 6, 1902. Her life was so beautiful and triumphant, so naturally imparting strength to others, and in its ending so happily sudden, that it would be almost an insult to her memory to recall dolorous circumstances connected with her departure and associate thoughts of sadness with so bright a being. Life, not death, is for all who loved her the significant reality. To dwell on the facts of parting is as inappropriate as to report how she closed her house when she was preparing for a sabbatical year in Europe.

Yet among what may be broadly called the living features of death two deserve attention: it no less than any other event is expressive of character, and the conditions under which it appears often give grounds for condemning or approving previous methods of life. To leave either of these points unnoticed, more particularly the latter, would render my account of Mrs. Palmer imperfect. I shall accordingly use her death as the occasion for considering some general questions about her: the brevity of her life, her physical constitution, the care of her health, and the cost of her large accomplishment.

Mrs. Palmer was an extremely busy woman. The amount of work she bore was enormous and the diversity of it no less remarkable. Since a large portion of it was connected with some sort of leadership, it brought upon her great responsibility and taxed her bodily and mental strength to the utmost. Her domestic cares were not less than those of ordinary women, nor less exquisitely performed. She did the usual amount of housekeeping, sewing, visiting, receiving guests, looking after the sick and poor, and attending social functions. In the occupations counted specifically feminine she even excelled. Yet after these were all beautifully accomplished there came those public duties to which she gave two thirds of her time. In these she carried almost the ordinary work of a college official, a minister, and a business man combined. And while it is true that until her marriage she was free from household cares, this advantage was offset by the grinding character of the tasks in school and college, and by the unlimited demands to which her dutiful nature there exposed her. On the whole it may be said that from girlhood to the grave, with only brief intervals after marriage, her powers were kept under incessant tension. Naturally then she was often judged harshly. Was not her career simply another instance of headlong and ill-regulated zeal? Did she not by example encourage repose-needing women to undertake what was excessive even for a man? Powers like hers should have been treated with respect and guarded. Was not her wastefulness sure to result in early collapse? And when her death before the age of fifty startled the many who needed her, these doubts were doubled and the inquiry was inevitable whether it would not have been wiser to continue longer at a slower pace? I hope every reader of my book has been asking these questions. This is the place to answer them.

No one would affirm that her life in college or in her early teaching was ideal. It contained twice too much work and only half enough refreshment. It was attended throughout by crushing anxieties. Had her health been properly regarded at this time, she might have eradicated some of the physical weaknesses she inherited and so have greatly lightened the labors of later years. That she did not do so, however, was not her fault. The exactions of those years she did not choose. They were laid upon her by poverty. She had an education to gain, a living to earn; and she accepted their hard conditions as cheerfully as have hundreds of other young men and women. I wonder that she passed through them with so little physical damage and drew from them such refinement and charm.

Nor do I see any signs of carelessness in the Wellesley time. During her teaching there the disturbed conditions inseparable from the starting of a new college overworked all its Faculty, utterly breaking down its leaders, — the founder, the president, and herself. She alone showed such sagacity in methods of restoration that she was soon able to return to work and accept the presidency; her chief hesitation in doing so being, as the letters I have printed show, the doubt whether she ought to expose herself to new exhaustion. Once having decided that the college was more important than herself, she was obliged to give herself wholly to its demands. Yet even then she studied protective measures. She kept a horse and took regular exercise; she was careful of food and sleep; at times of special fatigue she would spend a day or two at a solitary room in Boston; and as soon as a cottage could be built at Wellesley for housing a few girls, she removed from the great hall and sheltered herself in its comparative seclusion. On the whole, there were few means of protection available during this gloriously self-sacrificing period which she did not employ.

I speak of these matters somewhat in detail because, like most great workers, she attached much importance to the physical basis of life and constantly warned her girls against disregard of the laws of health. Yet it should also be said that she expected her life to be a short one and was ever solicitous how to effect what she desired within its brief compass. We have seen how the uncertainties of her college years led her to treat each of them as if it were to be her last; and something of the same feeling attended her through life, I hardly know why. Partly it came from her knowledge of the inherited dangers of her constitution; still more, I think, from her sense of the urgency of human needs, and such a recognition as Jesus had that those who would meet them must be ready to be consumed. But this was not all. There was besides a sort of presentiment which I could never fully explore or remove. It was seldom asserted, never argued; only when I would attempt to make some provision for her old age, I was always met by the quiet words, "You need n't

I shan't survive you. My life will be short." I think she was surprised that the end was deferred so long.

Expecting then a brief career, one might suppose she would have cleared it of all unnecessary toil and so have "saved her strength." But this popular phrase she utterly distrusted, and her life ought to do much to make that distrust more general. The notion that to each of us is allotted a definite amount of vigor, and that expenditure causes diminution of the total sum, she regarded as a pernicious mechanical superstition. It is certainly the common excuse for inaction, and more than anything else checks the full development of women. Idleness is in reality far more dangerous than work. It is in the nature of life to grow by exercise and, with proper care, to increase through outgo. The blacksmith does not enfeeble his arm by pounding; that is his method of enlarging its power. She believed continuous work to be conducive to health and she proved it so by practice. Beginning weak and working steadily, often unable to secure proper safeguards against exhaustion, she escaped all the ills from which idle women suffer, acquired remarkable hardihood, and almost every year found herself sturdier than before. If there is any one lesson which Mrs. Palmer's life preëminently teaches, it is the life-preserving influence of persistent, severe, and judiciously managed labor.

I have said that such judicious management was not fully possible until her marriage. Throughout the third period of her life, as I have divided it, her public services were largely of a sacrificial sort and were understood to have little reference to her own needs. But in her last fifteen years, in what I have called her fourth period, there was no such clash of interests. Though never more widely useful, she was then heartily enjoying the full exercise of disciplined powers. Culpable indeed she must have been if during these years she overworked.

On the whole, I do not think she did. Like everybody, she had her times of weariness. The accident described in my twelfth chapter brought permanent damage. But neither this nor any previous fatigue had any influence in shortening her life. She died of a rare disease, intus-susception of the intestine, a disease against which no precautions are possible. Its causes are totally unknown. Many physicians believe it to be congenital, and all those consulted agreed that nothing which she had done or left undone could in any way have hastened it. When the trouble began she was in excellent health, and in the intervals of its covert advance she was altogether free from disturbance. Of the many experienced surgeons summoned for diagnosis not one suspected danger till five days before she died, nor after they advised an operation did they see much chance of recovery.

Yet even then so hardy was she that she came through one of the severest operations known to surgery, lay painless and peaceful for three days, and would probably have survived had nature endowed her at birth with a full pulse. The circumstances of her death give strong confirmation to her gospel of work.

Yet in expounding that gospel I ought to make plain how much she excluded from it which ordinarily slips in. She seldom hurried, never worried, admitted no regrets for the past or anxieties for the future. Drudgery she abhorred, and consequently avoided too great single continuity on the one hand, and disjointed fragmentariness on the other. From these insidious dangers she was saved by habits of concentrated attention, by the deep interest she took in all she did, by such perception of its human bearings that no part of it became mechanical, by quick separation of the important and unimportant, by perpetual humor, and steady enthusiasm — the whole supplemented by a kind of natural vagrancy. She dropped work as easily as she took it up, and never acquired the fatal inability to stop. It was the whole-hearted character of that work which kept it sane and safe. Joy is protective. Where soul, mind, and strength are all engaged together, invigoration usually follows. It is the divided nature which lacerates; the hands in one place, the heart in another. Putting herself fully into her work, and freeing it from frictions, she made an amount that was appalling to others really beneficial.

But while certain peculiarities of her temperament thus prevented injury from work, others exposed her to it. She was ever easy to be entreated, and each new thing appeared with an altogether special claim. Every good woman is in danger of over-helpfulness. Recognizing this beautiful danger, after our marriage I constituted myself her watchdog and barked violently at whatever suspicious persons I saw approach. It pleases me to think that by such hostilities I cut off a quarter of her labors, the least important quarter. Though occasionally chafing under the restraint, she on the whole saw my usefulness and rewarded me with adequate thanks.

If then this is a sufficient account of that curious diligence which might easily be supposed to have induced her comparatively early death, it only remains to state briefly the circumstances under which her life closed, especially those which most reveal her character.

In 1902, when a Sabbatical Year became due me, we were neither of us inclined to use it. Never had home seemed so attractive, nor our employments so engrossing. But in the past we had derived such benefit from these periodic relaxations that, not daring to reject this one altogether, we decided to accept the first part of it and to resume work in the middle of the year. Even then we lingered at Boxford through the summer and did not sail till the first of October. Some petty circumstances of our departure are perhaps characteristic enough to deserve mention.

We were to sail on Wednesday morning. During the preceding week I could not induce Mrs. Palmer to pack. That was our last week in Boxford, and we must enjoy it. When Monday came, we set about the business in earnest; but soon she wandered out under the peach tree, and came back reporting that some of the peaches were ripe, and I must get one she had noticed. I did so, and she declared it delicious. It would be a shame to leave such fruit to perish. We might take a little rest from packing and put up a few jars for winter. So we sat merrily down on the piazza and began peeling peaches. On one excuse and another I was sent back to the tree for more, till we had disposed of a bushel. Then the full absurdity of the situation came over me, and I said, "What fools we are! With all this work on hand, to sit through a morning peeling peaches! As if we could eat a bushel of peaches next year!" "Next year?" she answered. "Nonsense! They will be good for years to come, and the little packing is easily managed." And so it proved. She provided for my table long after she had left it, and time enough was found during the packing for two other considerable events. Tuesday afternoon we spent at the wedding of a friend; and Tuesday morning a young relative from the great house crossed the lawn to say that a young man in Cambridge had just written her a letter which promised something similar in the future for herself. Mrs. Palmer was all sympathy at once. We must have that young man here immediately. I must ride to the village and telephone orders for him to appear that night. And so it happened that our last evening at home was given to a rejoicing pair, and the trunks were seemingly left to pack themselves. But this they did. On Wednesday morning they stood quite ready, and nothing was afterwards missed from them which Europe required.

Two young friends joined us in Boston: Miss S. to be our companion throughout, and Mr. M. for the first month only. An important fifth member of our party was the old English poet, George Herbert, whose works I was then editing and whose embroidered phrases were constantly on our lips. On landing in England, and after the usual few days at the Lakes, we put ourselves under his guidance, following him to all the places where he lived from birth to death. Many of these places we had visited before, but a few literary "finds" now made in them gave Mrs. Palmer much pleasure. So did a little stay in Oxford with some old friends. London gave her the magnificent pageant of King Edward acknowledging his recovery from recent illness; gave her, too, its National Gallery and the music at St. Paul's. About the first of November, Mr. M. leaving us, we crossed to Paris. Here we found our old rooms occupied, but were able to establish ourselves close at hand in an apartment at 67 Avenue Marceau. It is a wide, clean, and sunny street, the only objection to this new home being that it was larger and more magnificent than was our usual habit. But we closed its great reception room, with the mirrors and gilded furniture, and gathered about the open fire in the library. Here our little Marie served our meals; here during most of the mornings and evenings Mrs. Palmer sewed, wrote, or listened; and in the afternoons renewed her old pleasure in the Louvre, the river, Notre Dame, and the Théatre Français. Sundays were poorer than during earlier visits because of the death of the great Protestant preacher, Bersier. She counted him inferior only to Phillips Brooks.

But she had the little excursions which she always enjoyed. One sunny day we spent at Amiens Cathedral; one at St. Denis; and one evening on reading the paper she exclaimed, "To-day is All Saints' Day, and seventy thousand people have been at Père la Chaise. To-morrow there will be as many more. We must go." "But why," I said, "go where there is a crowd?" "Why, so as to be with people and join them in decorating the graves." We had never visited Père la Chaise before; but she was happy in climbing the flower-lined Rue Roquette, in hunting out the monuments of those she knew, in watching the funeral observances, so unlike those of her own land, and especially in mingling with the mourning multitude. As she approached the gate, a girl offered her violets. She bought a bunch, saying she would carry them to Héloïse, whom she admired as a great administrator no less than as an ardent woman. She found the tomb where the stone lovers lie, and tossed the violets over the railing. That night, meditating by the fireside, she remarked, "I like cremation better. Not that I would insist on it against the wishes of friends. Burial concerns the living more than the dead. But I hope I may be cremated." Such were the instructions I received only a month before I went with her for the second time to Père la Chaise.

During much of that month she was not ill, but merely ailing. From time to time she was able to go about freely, and between the attacks of seeming indigestion to be as well as ever. The last occasion on which she went out was in response to a request for an address at a girls' school. I am told she was never more delightful, though only three weeks later that school sat with me at her funeral. There followed this address a week under the doctor's charge, with apparent cure; another, of fresh outbreak and of consultation with three eminent physicians, all perplexed; in another still came the decision to operate, the private hospital, the death. During her last fortnight she lay most of the time, patient and interested, in the library, and had me read her two books which had just been sent, President Hyde's little volume, "Jesus' Way," and Quiller-Couch's "Oxford Book of Poetry." She continued to discuss my problems in Herbert; and when the Boston papers arrived, I must quickly discover the home news and report it all. To the last she did not lose that mental eagerness. A spasm of pain would overwhelm her, leaving her for a moment unconscious; then the eyes would unclose and she would say, "There, that is gone; and what did they do on the School Board?" She lived fully, so long as she drew breath.

On Wednesday of the last week the doubtful doctors came early, and after consultation ordered an operation for that noon; they did not conceal from her that it would probably be fatal, for in all the necessary examinations she had been the coolest and helpfulest of the company. They leaving us at nine, we had an hour together before she was removed.

And then appeared for the last time that strange combination of clear intelligence and emotional ardor, of sweet womanliness and attention to business, which ever distinguished her. Her fearless wise talk had even its usual humorous turns. As the door closed, she bade me fetch a package of papers and handed me back a little group. These were her engagements for the winter. I must write to these people and not let them be disappointed. Then there were the friends at home, to each of whom something was sent; and I must watch over her parents and sister. "Bobby will miss me," she said. He was her godson. I must not spend the summer in Boxford. Later ones would be good there, but this year I had better carry out an engagement to lecture in California. She thought she understood my work. I had promised her a little book on ethics. Could I do that in a year? And then I must not allow anything to intervene till our Herbert was published. That would require two years more; and so it did. Beyond that, nobody could foresee. But there would be our two colleges, our boys and girls — work enough to keep me busy, work too which had interested us both. She could think of no last words to say; our whole lives had spoken those. We knew each other's deep love; and I must treat myself honorably, allowing no doubts or regrets to come. "Call our faithful Marie and give her this dress. And now," she said, "you must go to the hospital and have the room ready when the ambulance arrives."

I had some fears about the hospital. Sanitarily excellent as it was, and containing the best skill in France, its nurses were black-robed nuns with white head-bands. Her room was consecrated to John the Baptist, and an image of the saint stood by her head. Formalism in religion was peculiarly obnoxious to her. The simplicity prized everywhere else she counted essential in her approaches to God. It struck me therefore as bizarre that this widely loved American and Protestant should die almost alone among Roman Catholics, persons who knew no English words and could comprehend still less the conditions of mind behind them. But all my fears were set at rest the next morning. As I entered, her face was all aglow over "this blessed place where the air seems full of religion, and one feels entirely free and at ease." She reminded me of her two previous hospital experiences, but neither so satisfactory as this. I had to check her eager whisperings and to say that we must use whatever strength she had pretty skilfully if we would celebrate our wedding-day a fortnight hence. With a gay smile she answered that together we had pulled ourselves through many tight places, and we really might cheat the doctors yet. Of course she endeared herself to doctors and nurses. When early on Saturday morning the breath quietly stopped, the attending sister broke into sobs. I asked, "Est-ce qu'elle est morte?" "Morte, Monsieur!" she cried, "Mais qu'elle était une femme exceptionelle!"

Would she have had more chance for life, or less suffering, if the inevitable catastrophe had befallen her in America? Certainly one would have selected these circumstances for her death as little as he would have chosen most of the other severities of that life which still all called good. Events must be judged in relation to character. Judging so, I think those of her ending fortunate. She was attended by the highest skill; had every comfort of home, food, and care; her admirable servant would have died for her at any minute; she held her consciousness to the last, making the business of dying as brief as she had always hoped it might be; and by her banishment was saved from the inquiries, anxieties, and lamentations of friends. I cannot imagine a greater distress to that tender heart than would have been the sufferings of others on her account. Only the Sunday before she died she reproached me for writing to a friend that she was not quite well. But though no regrets are proper for the manner of her death, who can contemplate the fact of it and not call the world irrational if out of deference to a few particles of disordered matter it excludes so fair a spirit?

XV

CHARACTER

On returning from Europe I was asked to allow a service to be held in Cambridge in memory of Mrs. Palmer. I gladly did so, and a large company of her friends assembled in the chapel of Harvard College on January 31, 1903. Every part of the service was in charge of those who had known and loved her. Few strangers were in the audience. The ushers were teachers and students who had been much in her home. A chorus of Harvard men and another of Wellesley girls furnished the music, singing her hymn, "The Tempest," and others which were especially dear to her. Professor Peabody read the Scripture and offered prayer; and four college presidents — Presidents Angell, Hazard, Tucker, and Eliot — made addresses. At the beginning of the programme, as at the beginning of this book, was placed Mr. Gilder's exquisite lament; and at the end, some lines adapted from Richard Crashaw, a poet of whom she had long been fond.

The addresses on this occasion explore Mrs. Palmer's character with great acuteness, beauty, and affection. Each of the four speakers, looking back

Last Portrait

on the life, tells what he has seen in it. Perhaps I had better do so too. Now that the story of her deeds is done, and we can no more watch the development of her career, it may be well to summarize the qualities disclosed. I at least love to linger over her several traits no less than to observe how each was glorified by its connection with the rest. My reader too will be glad to have them passed in review, if that review is brief, frank, reverent, and systematic. A kind of moral index may appropriately close this book. Successively then I will examine her physical, temperamental, intellectual, moral, and religious structure.

She was of medium height, a little below the average, and in early life of slender build. At the time of her marriage she weighed but a hundred pounds. As she afterwards added some forty pounds to this, I made it my boast that there was about a third of her which I did not marry, but had made. Never strong, she was rarely ill, had great power of endurance, and was seldom shaken by sudden strain. I have said that her lungs were her weak part, and that from the time she went to college she had a constant cough. She always took cold easily. There may have been also some weakness of the heart, for her pulse was so faint that in her best health it was difficult to find it. But her step was elastic, her bearing erect, her enjoyment of the mere act of living incessant. She was sensitive to pain, and her keen perceptions of sight, touch, and taste brought her acute pleasure. All her movements were rapid; as, however, she had herself completely under control and was quite without nervousness, one received from her the impression of calm. When she sat, she sat still. A favorite posture was that of listening, the body slightly inclined forward and resting on the fore part of her chair.

Her face drew instant attention. When she was present it was as difficult to look at anything else as to turn the eye away from a flickering fire. One hardly asked if the face was beautiful, so immediate was the sense of its nobility, its abounding life, and its searching personal appeal. Above the large, dark, hazel eyes grew luxuriant hair of the same color, curling low down over the wide brow and everywhere trying to free itself from restraint for play about the shapely head. The cheek bones were strongly marked, as in Scotch faces; the nose straight and not large, the full lips slightly parted. The chin and lower face had no particular form, but were moulded by herself into endless varieties of expression. Indeed the whole face varied so widely that photographs taken on the same day might easily be mistaken for those of different women. Shifting lights flashed under the skin, as in portraits by Leonardo. By printing several of her pictures, each in itself unsatisfactory, I hope to show something of this baffling diversity.

In 1890 Abbott Thayer painted her portrait for Wellesley College; and in 1892 Anne Whitney carved her bust. The portrait, a young girl dreaming on the future of Wellesley, is charmingly idealized, but hardly reports her actual features. So mobile a face too is peculiarly unsuited to the rigidity of stone or bronze. Yet each artist has represented certain aspects of her delightfully. A monument interpreting her work, designed by Daniel Chester French, has been placed in Wellesley College Chapel.

Passing beyond physical aspects and looking more closely at the woman herself, we come upon those half unconscious dispositions which are conveniently grouped together under the name of temperament. These represent our emotional habits rather than our deliberate purposes. They are largely inherited, or the natural result of conduct long gone by; and while highly distinctive of each of us, hardly possess a moral quality. They are the raw material out of which character is formed, and become good or bad according to their use. As mere things of nature, unsanctioned by will, they are more often associated with our weakness than our strength. Yet however imperfect they may severally be, and even open one by one to disparagement, together they form the groundwork of the intellectual and moral life. No man is strong or much prized who is not richly temperamental.

Mrs. Palmer's temperament was an ardent one. She entered intensely into all she did. While astonishingly responsive, and answering with almost equal readiness the call of a bird or a human soul, she was for the moment absorbed in each. Persons easily played upon by things around are likely after a time to find all trivial. But for her everything held its importance, and even in repetition was fresh. She had strong likes and dislikes, though there were many more of the former, because under that penetrating eye each thing or person was pretty sure to disclose points on which kindly interest might fasten. But when she came upon a case of perversity, or what at the moment she mistook for this, her indignation was fierce. Shortly after her death one who knew her well remarked to me, on reading a eulogy of her, that the writer had missed his mark through not mentioning her power of scorn. And I perceived that he was right; scorn was an essential factor in her. Few illustrated better than this tender and sympathetic woman what our Scriptures mean by "the wrath of the lamb." There were persons for whom she felt a positive aversion.

Generally, however, like most of those engaged in constructive work, she was optimistic, sanguine of good in all, whether persons or events. Most things have a bright and dark side. Her instinct was for brightness. Being resourceful, too, and delighting to push a path through unknown regions, she readily discovered in any human situation, however unpropitious, some means of access to the good she sought. The world was her playground. Obstacles, loss, stubborn material, slender means, suffering, failure even, only quickened her adroitness and brought greater enjoyment to the game of life. A hardened optimist I have elsewhere called her; and probably her spirit of persistent buoyancy is about the richest gift which nature ever bestows on a traveller through our perplexing world. She knew it to be a means of power, prized it, cultivated it, and seldom allowed work and play to become dissociated. Humor was used unceasingly to oil the machinery of life. No occasion was too grave for a good story. I have heard of a little girl who on being reproved for laughter during prayers queried, "Why, can't God take a joke?" Mrs. Palmer thought He could; and while deeply reverent, obliged serious and topsy-turvy things to live in pretty close intimacy.

Yet when moods of depression came, as come to all they will, she was perfectly frank in expressing them. They are openly announced in several of the letters which I have printed. Indeed I sometimes thought that such moods, like all else in her world, furnished a kind of fresh matter for amusement, they were let loose with such unnecessary warmth. Usually they sprang from fatigue. Of this ignominious root she seemed herself half conscious, aware therefore that the abuse plentifully distributed to all the world and its inhabitants belonged not so much to it as to her own infirmity. But this reflection, if it came, in no wise abated either her vehemence or her sensible conduct. There were few of those she cared for against whom she did not occasionally fulminate; and artificial though these denunciations were, and little as they affected her devotion to their objects, they held close to fact, were incisive, and as entertainingly exuberant as her more frequent outbursts of praise. They were in reality mere explosions, temperamental modes of blowing off steam, practised often when alone; for she had the habit of talking much to herself. But she knew the difference between a mood and a judgment, kept each in its place, and put the former swiftly by as soon as occasion required. If she happened to grow weary of a friend, she would drop him for a time — often, I suspect, to his considerable perplexity; but at any moment of his need he would find that all her love was warm and waiting. "Life's a chore," she would say as she trudged off promptly to a disagreeable committee meeting. "I want to do something," was a frequent cry when one of these black moods was upon her. "Shall we play a game, or have some reading, or will you lie down and rest?" "No, no! I want to *do* something." And then I must contrive an escapade, the crazier the better, to clear away the fretting deposit of the day; after which she would hurry back joyfully to work and people, and with all the more eagerness for having temporarily put them by.

It is not necessary to speak further of her extreme diligence, which has been illustrated on every page of this book. I will merely reiterate two qualifications of it; that while skilful in using fragments of time, she seldom appeared in haste, nor ever lost the ability to be idle. Yet most industrious persons are orderly also, and this she was not. She often lamented it pathetically; on her last departure for Europe, for example, bidding her sister go to a certain closet, in case she did not return, and destroy all its contents, because she would lose my respect if I came upon such a rubbish heap. For sorting things as she used them, and condemning some, her incapacity was extreme. But I think the disorderliness was chiefly confined to two matters: letters, which have always a fragrant personality about them, and which before her marriage had been generally cared for by her secretary; and then other articles to which her tenacious affections clung, articles many and miscellaneous. She liked to keep things, regardless of their use. A flower given by a friend, a pebble picked up on a significant occasion, an old school-book, a concert programme, a fragment of dress worn at some festival, while acknowledged to be much in the way, were exempt from destruction, and gradually filled many a drawer and chest. But her business habits were models of exactitude, and about her rooms and person there could never be anything in the least untidy. Of course her writing-table was always a complete chaos; and a certain mode of increasing that chaos may be mentioned, a pretty way she had of dealing with letters which could not immediately be answered. She would address an envelope to the writer, stamp it, and tossing it on the general pile, would appear to win an easy conscience for a fairly extended delay.

Perhaps in closing this sketch of her temperament I should mention again its strangely quickening quality, its tendency to call forth as by a kind of magic the best powers of whomever she came near. By identifying herself with those about her she stirred their imitative will. But as this occult process has been pretty fully described elsewhere, I will here merely cite two contrasted instances of it. The first is that of a scholar and author, eminent in this country and abroad. He writes: "When I last saw Mrs. Palmer I was in a hopeless state, caring little what I did, especially as regards writing. I never mentioned this to her, but with that marvelous instinct of hers I think she perceived it. At any rate she began at once to kindle me, and before I knew what was happening I was afire to do a man's work again. It is a deep regret that the book she prompted, the most elaborate and influential I have written, her death prevented me from laying in her hands and saying, 'This have I done because you helped me to do it by casual words of encouragement.'"

The second letter is from a farmer's wife: "She gave so much of herself to every living thing! To meet her at the Boxford Station in the morning made the whole day bright. If she passed me in the late afternoon on the long hill, she seemed the fairest object in all that stretch of sweet country. I remember, too, how beautiful she was at the communion table, with the uncovered head, in her summer dresses. Even her pictures speak. I cut one from the Boston paper that brought the news of her death. It is pinned on the wall over my table. I often look at it and promise, 'I will be a better woman, Mrs. Palmer, because you have lived.' And then out of the great speaking eyes comes a merry glance that shows me she understands."

Hitherto we have considered merely the instinctive sides of her, — her temperament, habits, the natural machinery which kept her in motion while her intelligence was engaged with other things. But that intelligence itself claims attention. It had the same swiftness which characterized her throughout, conducting her usually at once to the heart of a subject and allowing her to waste little time on side issues. Her immediate judgments were sagacious judgments. In discussion she caught the point quickly, would summarize lucidly an argument she had heard or a book she had read, and in dealing with all sorts of people perceived by a kind of instinct their state of mind and quickly adapted to it whatever she had to say. I have no need to enlarge on the versatility of her mind; but will call attention once more to the intellectual patience with which she pursued distant and large ends, and also to her constant preference of original and creative work to that of mere routine.

Circumstances in the middle of her life may possibly have somewhat changed her mental bias. When she went to college she was bent on becoming a scholar, and for a time was drawn most strongly toward mathematics and Greek, two subjects as remote as any from practical affairs. Gradually history claimed her, and in it she began studies for the doctorate. At this time, I judge, her aim was specialization, scientific scholarship. But in this country any one who has both scholarly and administrative talents is pretty sure to be called on to swamp the former in the latter, particularly if he has his own bread to earn. From the time she took charge of a school the practical side of her nature was uppermost. Perhaps it always had been. Though afterwards for two years she taught history skilfully at

Wellesley, she was even then more occupied with guiding girls and organizing a college than with pure scholarship. Somebody said of her at this time that she was born to rule a nation by a turn of her little finger. So it continued through subsequent life: the practical reason, and not the theoretic, remained her field. It was always the concrete thing, the particular individual, the single institution with its special problems, which engaged her. In what masterly fashion she dealt with them I will not repeat. My readers are already sufficiently familiar with her sure observation, grasp, constructive power, ingenuity, fair-mindedness, and estimate of values — all qualities implying intellect of a high order. To me the distinguishing marks of her mind, in all its forms of outgo, are its speed, ease, and sanity.

Probably all her intellectual powers got effectiveness and were prevented from damaging their owner by that specialized control of attention which is frequently seen in successful administrators. As each separate person, topic, or situation came forward for judgment, she gave it her whole mind; and then, after sentence pronounced, from her whole mind also it disappeared. Such minds work in closed compartments and admit few straggling thoughts. At times of business she did not look much before or after, but straight into. This concentration I regard as one of the surest indications of intellectual force.

In testing practical power we may well ask how long can a person hold the attention firmly and freshly on a single subject, and then how fully can he give it its discharge? In my narrative this ability to switch on and switch off has been amply illustrated.

Her moral nature was grounded in sympathy. Beginning early, the identification of herself with others grew into a constant habit, of unusual range and delicacy. I have shown how in her childhood each member of the family was called on to contribute whatever he had to the common stock, how each felt himself responsible for all, and separate interests were unknown. This enforced public sense, behind which she did not at that time go, became in later years a conscious principle guiding her life, and one which she longed to see guiding the lives of all. To get anything at the cost of another was impossible for her; to keep anything which another might need, painful. She suffered with those whom she saw suffer. Righteousness is, after all, merely the daily love of man — of man in his divinity, weakness, aspirations, errors, interests, and idiosyncracies. This Jesus announced, St. Francis preached, and all great moralists have urged. To it Mrs. Palmer had habituated herself until it imparted elevation and sweetness to her commonest acts. Its working will most easily be seen in a few trivial instances.

A poor woman of Boxford tells me that she was leaning over her gate one evening, watching for her husband's return, when Mrs. Palmer passed by. As usual, she stopped to talk. Incidentally she learned that the good wife's soup for supper was waiting to be made till the farmer should bring a couple of turnips from the village. Mrs. Palmer walked on, but soon appeared again, turnips in hand. The soup could be started.

One summer a young bride came to Boxford. In calling on her, Mrs. Palmer wanted to hear every detail of the wedding and to see the beautiful clothes. Into the enjoyment of these fineries she entered with unbounded zest, but said at the close, "Don't wear them too often here. Plain dressing is best for the country; and clothes that put a distance between you and other people are not nice." With such fragrant trifles her daily ways were strewn.

Being so sympathetic, she naturally enjoyed everybody and condescended to none. Whether she mingled with scholars and business men, with children and society women, with lawyers, school-girls, country folk, or criminals, she took them just as they stood, found them all vividly interesting, and they found her not less so. When in close contact with wrongdoers, I think she seldom censured them, even in her own mind, but felt the naturalness of their case, the pity of it, the wealth of life they were losing, and the longing — soon felt by them too — for bridges of return. In one of his parables Jesus warns his disciples against plucking up tares in fields of grain. The roots of the two are so intertwined, he thinks, that a hasty pull at the poorer may easily damage the better. Apparently some such view made her tolerant of evil. To its eradication she gave little heed, preferring rather to fertilize the good until it should be strong enough to crowd out inferior growths.

Most persons will agree that sympathy is the predominantly feminine virtue, and that she who lacks it cannot make its absence good by any collection of other worthy qualities. In a true woman sympathy directs all else. To find a virtue equally central in a man we must turn to truthfulness or courage. These also a woman should possess, as a man too should be sympathetic; but in her they take a subordinate place, subservient to omnipresent sympathy. Within these limits the ampler they are, the nobler the woman.

I believe Mrs. Palmer had a full share of both these manly excellences, and practised them in thoroughly feminine fashion. She was essentially true, hating humbug in all its disguises. Being a keen observer, she knew a fact when she saw it and did not juggle with herself by calling things what they are not. Her love of plainness and distaste for affectation were forms of veracity. But in a narrative of hers one got much besides plain realities. These had their significance heightened by her eager emotion, and their picturesqueness by her happy artistry. In merry moods her fantastic exaggerations were delightful. Of course the warmth of her sympathy cut off all inclination to falsehood for its usual selfish purpose. But against generous untruth she was not so well guarded. Kindness was the first thing. In dealing with a trembling soul, if the bluntness of reality would hurt, its edges were smoothed. Tact too, once become a habit, made adaptation to the mind addressed a constant concern. She had extraordinary skill in stuffing kindness with truth; and into a resisting mind could without irritation convey a larger bulk of unwelcome fact than any one I have known. But that insistence on colorless statement which in our time the needs of trade and science have made current among men, she did not feel. Lapses from exactitude which do not separate person from person she easily condoned.

Her courage was remarkable. President Eliot has selected this trait for special eulogy: "One of the most fascinating attributes of Mrs. Palmer was her courage. She was one of the bravest persons I ever saw, man or woman. Courage is a pleasing attribute in a tough, powerful, healthy man; it is perfectly delightful in a delicate, tender woman." But this courage, extreme though it was, was also chiefly an expression of social loyalty, victorious over personal feeling. There was in it little of that blind push which knows no danger; she had her feminine fears. A cow, a mouse, a snake were objects of terror. I seldom went to walk in Paris that she did not warn me of the perils of street-crossings. She was sensitive to the judgments of others, and shrank from having anything in her dress, speech, or behavior remarked as "queer." To be conspicuous was disagreeable. But such timidities were altogether set aside the moment aid could be given. In the public interest or in helping those she loved she never faltered. No difficulty, risk, or misconception stopped her serene advance. Her mind appeared to gain additional clearness and resolve in times of danger, and the dependence of persons on her to be a chief source of strength. Kant declares that in the voice of duty we hear the assurance, "You can, because you ought." Mrs. Palmer believed this fully. Wherever there was human need she turned without measuring powers or preferences. The time of her sister's death, her presidency at Wellesley, the busy years of Cambridge were crowded with cases of such easy hardihood. Two little instances from private life will show how exquisitely love could embolden her.

In 1896 I was ordered to undergo a serious surgical operation. On leaving home for the Boston hospital

I charged Mrs. Palmer not to visit me till the following noon, when the operation would be over. But she timed her coming so as to arrive while I was still in the surgeon's hands. She wanted an opportunity quietly to inspect my room. About it she arranged pleasant articles from our home, and then discovered that my pillow was not what she approved. Hurrying back to Cambridge, she seized the long pillow from my bed, crossed Boston with it in her arms — the four miles requiring a change of electric cars and a considerable walk — reached my room before I was brought in, and when I awoke she was sitting by my head, which rested on the sacred pillow. Subsequently I asked if she had not found it disagreeable to expose herself on streets and in public conveyances with so unusual a burden; but she seemed hardly to comprehend my question. She had been thinking of my comfort and had not noticed smiling observers.

A few years later she herself was in a low state, and I could get no exact account of what the matter was. One Sunday, as I knelt beside her in the Boxford church, I saw a tear drop to the floor. Gaily, however, she went off to Boston on Monday, saying her doctor had promised full details of the case that day. Toward evening I received a note announcing that she was to be operated upon on the following morning. Knowing that I was pledged to a difficult piece of writing, she had kept her trouble to herself so long as concealment was possible.

Between a life which so embodies those of its fellows and a life of religion there is little difference; but there is a little, and hers was a specifically religious nature. In every call of human need she heard the voice of God, summoning her to free his children from selfishness and woe. The love of God, it has been well said, is devotion to duty intensified in intellectual clearness and in emotional strength by the conviction that its aim is also that of a great personality. This courage-bringing conviction she had. All her morality was therefore touched with a divine emotion. Her aims were unified. In solitude and suffering she was not alone. She knew that the stars in their courses shone on her designs, and accessible love throbbed through all things.

In my third chapter I have explained how this clear consciousness of personal friendship with the Ruler of all began in the perplexing exaltations of the Windsor period. The larger love was revealed through the limitations of the smaller. But the consecration then made was no temporary affair. It bore the strains of more than thirty years, being renewed in the Sunday schools of Ann Arbor, at her sister's bedside, by spiritual ministrations at Wellesley, and in the busy peace of the Cambridge home. But hers was a free soul. Into her religion no dread entered. She rejoiced in the Lord and in the power of his might. And just as her intercourse with her fellow men was directed by sympathy for their needs and interests, so did a kind of sympathy with God shape her devotion. He was her steady companion, so naturally a part of her hourly thought that she attached little consequence to specific occasions of intercourse. While she entered heartily into church services, even when of a pretty rude order, her Sundays hardly differed from other days. She had no fixed times of prayer or devout reading, and in general attached little importance to pious proprieties.

Prizing too spiritual diversity and bold with divine affections, she welcomed every species of earnest seeking after God. With all sorts of believers and unbelievers she associated with equal freedom, and felt God stirring in them all. Only two religious animosities did I ever detect in her. She was uncomfortable with those who make of religion a thing apart, an affair of performance and ritual; and again with the negationists and minimizers, those who seek to reduce religion to its lowest terms, questioning its poetry and timid over a creed. Her own creed was clear and strong, being that of the orthodox faith. In ideal manhood she saw the complete revelation of God. Reverently therefore she turned to Jesus of Nazareth and sought to make her life, like his, both human and divine.

Such was the woman of whom these pages treat — such, but oh how different! I am painfully conscious of my inability to revitalize so abounding a being. The life-blood is gone. A person once dead can hardly be made to walk again, certainly not by analytic me. In order to be less inadequate I have added to the earlier chapters, where she was moving through affairs, this summary of her more important traits. Yet such a precise and abstract statement belittles anew. The qualities we admired in her, taken singly, were fortunately not rare. Others possess them, possess them often in higher degree. Only their combination was remarkable. In her single person she harmonized what is commonly conflicting; so that while she conveyed rather unusually the impression of being made all in one piece, he who set out to describe her found himself obliged to contradict in each new sentence whatever he had asserted of her in his old. Such was her wealthy unity, the despair of him who would portray. Perhaps this is merely to say that she was very much of a woman. At any rate, so it was: so simple, yet so elusive was her blended nature.

And because of its combined variety and firmness that nature contained some provision for all; nor was it ever closed to any. She seemed built for bounty, and held nothing back. Gaily she went forth throughout her too few years, scattering happiness up and down neglected ways. A fainting multitude flocked around to share her wisdom, peace, hardihood, devoutness, and merriment; and more easily afterwards accommodated themselves to their lot. Strength continually went forth from her. She put on righteousness and it clothed her, and sound judgment was her daily crown. Each eye that saw her blessed her; each ear that heard her was made glad.

Hark hither, reader, will't thou see
Nature her own physician be.
Will't see a soul all her own wealth,
Her own music, her own health;
A soul whose sober thought can tell
How to wear her garments well,
Her garments that upon her sit
(As garments should do) close and fit;
A well-cloth'd soul, that's not opprest
Nor chokt with what she should be drest,
But sheathèd in a crystal shrine,
Through which all her bright features shine;
A soul whose intellectual beams
No mists do mask, no lazy steams;
A happy soul, that all the way
To heaven hath a summer's day;
Whose latest and most leaden hours
Fall with soft wings, please with gay flowers;
And when life's sweet fable ends
This soul and body part like friends;
No quarrels, murmurs, no delay;
A kiss, a sigh, and so away.

Adapted from RICHARD CRASHAW.

DATES

1855, February 21. Born at Colesville, New York.
1862–64. Father at Albany Medical School.
1864. Family moves to Windsor.
1865. Windsor Academy.
1872. Michigan University.
1875. Ottawa High School.
1876. B. A. Michigan. Geneva Lake Seminary.
1877–79. Saginaw High School.
1878. Family moves to Saginaw. Called to Wellesley.
1879. Stella Freeman dies. Professor of History at Wellesley.
1880. Severe illness.
1881. Mr. Durant dies. Acting President of Wellesley College.
1882. President of Wellesley and Ph.D. Michigan. Collegiate Alumnæ Association.
1884. In England.
1885. Norumbega Cottage.
1887. Litt. D. Columbia. Marries and moves to Cambridge.
1888. Trustee of Wellesley College.
1888–89. In Europe.
1889. Woman's Home Missionary Society. Massachusetts State Board of Education.

1891. Woman's Education Association.

1891. Board of Managers of World's Fair. Portrait painted.

1892. Bust carved. University of Chicago.

1894. Quincy Street, Cambridge. Endowment for Radcliffe College.

1895–96. In Europe.

1898. Bicycle Accident.

1900. International Institute for Girls in Spain. Bradford Academy.

1902. Death.